Allen Wilcox

QP lst 15⁰⁰

D0742657

Portmanteau Dictionary

Portmanteau Dictionary

*Blend Words in the
English Language, Including
Trademarks and Brand Names*

by

Dick Thurner

McFarland & Company, Inc., Publishers
Jefferson, North Carolina, and London

British Library Cataloguing-in-Publication data are available

Library of Congress Cataloguing-in-Publication Data

Thurner, Dick, 1950–
    The portmanteau dictionary : blend words in the English language,
including trademarks and brand names / by Dick Thurner.
      p. cm.
    Includes bibliographical references.
    ISBN 0-89950-687-9 (lib. bdg. : 50# alk. paper) ∞
    1. English language—Compound words—Dictionaries.   2. English
language—Etymology—Dictionaries. I. Title.
PE1175.T54 1993
423'.1—dc20   92-51011
                                         CIP

©1993 Dick Thurner. All rights reserved

Manufactured in the United States of America

McFarland & Company, Inc., Publishers
  Box 611, Jefferson, North Carolina 28640

CONTENTS

v

INTRODUCTION

Blend: A word composed of parts of two words, all of
one word and part of another, or two entire words,
characterized invariably in the latter case and frequently
in the two former cases by the single occurrence of one
or more sounds or letters that appear in both the component words. — *Webster's Third New International
Dictionary.*

The English language's reputation as a durable, resilient, "living
language" can be attributed to a process of evolutionary change that
continually provides the English-speaking world with a seemingly inex-
haustible supply of new words. Among the varied means by which
these new words are formed, one of the most popular and versatile is
the *portmanteau* or *blend word.*

Portmanteaus are distinguished from other types of compound
words by the fact that they blend together shared characteristics of their
component words. Common varieties of the portmanteau word include
those blending the initial sounds or syllables of one word with the last
of another, as in *anecdotage* or *guesstimate*; those merging like-
sounding words to create portmanteaus which are also puns, as in *shampagne*; or those which incorporate one complete and formerly separate
word within another, as in *metrollopis.*

Any one of these examples could be described as a typical portmanteau word, since each is a blending of two words into one. But
apart from these "typical" portmanteaus, there are also a number of
other variations of such blended words in English. For example, some
blended words may combine elements from more than two words, as
in *compushency* (compulsion + push + urgency), while others use conventional relationships between words to create entirely new expressions, as in *Uncle Tomahawk.*

And, while visual portmanteaus such as *shampagne* need to be seen in print to be appreciated, others depend primarily on blended *sounds* to express their meanings. These *onomatopoeic blends* derive from root words that may have themselves been imitations of natural sounds, which were then blended into forms that act to enhance or intensify the original words' sound and sense.

Thus, the act of striking a blow, often described by imitative words such as *bang* or *smash*, may also by expressed by a blend such as the equally emphatic *bash*, a process once described by Martin Gardner as a tendency of blended words to "take care of the sounds and allow the sense to take care of itself." American language scholar Louise Pound has suggested that sound elements from as many as a half dozen words could be cited as likely sources for a blend such as *splurge*, which may number *splash, splatter, splutter, surge* and *large* among its ancestors.

For centuries, this tendency to compress a language by combining words has been one of the principal trends in the evolution of English; the widespread use of contractions and the modern-day proliferation of acronymic words are some other examples of this trend. Earlier instances could be cited as well: examples of word blends have been found in Old English manuscripts dating from as early as the 7th century. Blended words coined either by accident or design have been turning up ever since, and have appeared in such venerable works of English literature as Spenser's *Faerie Queene* and the plays of William Shakespeare, as well as in the writings of John Dryden, Samuel Richardson, Herman Melville, Sir Walter Scott, Charles Dickens, Virginia Woolf, H. L. Mencken, Sinclair Lewis, James Joyce, Robert Frost, Aldous Huxley and Samuel Beckett.

It is important to acknowledge the long history of the portmanteau word, since a relatively recent English writer by the name of Charles Dodgson—better known as Lewis Carroll—has often been erroneously credited with its invention. He was not the first to use such words, but Lewis Carroll does deserve much of the credit for popularizing blends as an important element of modern English.

As a mathematics lecturer at Oxford, Carroll demonstrated a mathematician's keen appreciation for ingenious puzzles and economical expressions of thought, and his many experiments with word games are tokens of his lifelong fascination with language. In puzzles such as the double acrostic, a forerunner of the modern crossword puzzle, in which words are joined by shared letters, and *Doublets*, a word game he sold to *Vanity Fair* magazine, in which the challenge is to link two words together by interposing words differing from each other by only one letter, Carroll cleverly explored the possibilities of allowing words to serve as building blocks for other words.

His love of elaborate wordplay may be most evident in the poem "Jabberwocky," which appeared in *Through the Looking Glass* in 1872, and is still considered one of the greatest nonsense poems in English literature:

> Twas brillig, and the slithy toves
> Did gyre and gimble in the wabe:
> All mimsy were the borogoves,
> And the mome raths outgrabe.
>
> "Beware the Jabberwock, my son!
> The jaws that bite, the claws that catch!
> Beware the Jubjub bird, and shun
> The frumious Bandersnatch!"
>
> He took his vorpal sword in hand:
> Long time the manxome foe he sought—
> So rested he by the Tumtum tree,
> And stood awhile in thought.
>
> And, as in uffish thought he stood,
> The Jabberwock, with eyes of flame,
> Came whiffling through the tulgey wood,
> And burbled as it came!
>
> One, two! One, two! And through and through
> The vorpal blade went snicker-snack!
> He left it dead, and with its head
> He went galumphing back.
>
> "And hast thou slain the Jabberwock?
> Come to my arms, my beamish boy!
> O frabjous day! Callooh! Callay!"
> He chortled in his joy.
>
> Twas brillig, and the slithy toves
> Did gyre and gimble in the wabe:
> All mimsy were the borogoves,
> And the mome raths outgrabe.

Based on a parody of traditional Anglo-Saxon heroic verse Carroll had written as a young man, the poem's peculiar form of invented language caused an immediate sensation. Many of Carroll's readers were agreeably entertained and yet baffled by it, responding to "Jabber-wocky" with a mixture of admiration and puzzlement. Some no doubt echoed the perplexity of Alice, the book's central character, who responds to the poem by saying, "Somehow it seems to fill my head with ideas—only I don't exactly know what they are!"

Carroll does provide an explanation of sorts in a later chapter of *Through the Looking Glass*. Alice is impressed by Humpty Dumpty's contention that a word can mean whatever one wants it to mean, so she asks him to explain the language of "Jabberwocky." He replies: "Well, slithy means lithe and slimy. Lithe is the same as active. You see, it's like a portmanteau—there are two meanings packed up into one word."

Lewis Carroll borrowed the name "portmanteau" from a particular style of luggage which had become extremely popular among travelers on the new railroads of that era. A portmanteau or "Gladstone" is a stiff leather case which opens down the middle like a book, combining two separate storage compartments in one traveling bag. The name stuck, despite the preference of most linguists for the term *blend*, and despite the number of alternatives which have been proposed ever since, including *centaur words, amalgams, mongrel words, brunch words, fusions,* and *telescope words*.

Carroll must have realized that Humpty Dumpty's remarks would hardly serve as an adequate explanation for the obscure language of "Jabberwocky," since he tried to explain the origin of these curious words again in the introduction to *The Hunting of the Snark*, published four years later:

> Humpty Dumpty's theory, of two meanings packed into one word like a portmanteau, seems to me the right explanation for all. For instance, take the two words "fuming" and "furious." Make up your mind that you will say both words, but leave it unsettled which you will say first. Now open your mouth and speak. If your thoughts incline ever so little towards "fuming," you will say "fuming-furious"; if they turn, by even a hair's breadth, towards "furious," you will say "furious-fuming"; but if you have that rarest of gifts, a perfectly balanced mind, you will say "frumious."

Whether the product of a balanced or unbalanced mind, Jabber-wocky words such as *slithy, chortle, burble* and *galumph* were quickly embraced by fashionable Victorian society, and were soon appearing in the works of Rudyard Kipling and other contemporary writers. Coining blend words became the smart and stylish thing to do, and a host of new blend words began appearing after the popular success of "Jabberwocky" including many now-familiar portmanteaus such as *brunch, electrocute, guesstimate, smog, travelogue* and *urinalysis.*

Why did Lewis Carroll enjoy such success in popularizing the portmanteau word? Perhaps the Victorian Age's rapid acceptance of blend words merely serves as an indicator of a growing appetite for new words in the English-speaking world of the 19th century.

Carroll's lifetime (1832–1898) spanned much of the new Industrial Age, when vast changes in virtually every aspect of British and American society were making unprecedented demands upon our language's ability to grow and adapt. As the pace of social and technological change continued to accelerate dramatically throughout the 19th century and into the 20th, the traditional academic method of fashioning new words from suitable Latin and Greek roots could not have met the challenge of providing all the new words which have entered the language since Carroll's day. Blends have provided a useful alternative or supplement to this process — especially since their reliance on source words from everyday English results in new expressions which are more apt to be quickly introduced, understood, and accepted into common use.

The nomenclature of virtually any modern-day technological field could be cited as evidence of this shift to non-academic, non-classical sources for new words. One particularly quirky example is the science of quantum mechanics, a highly esoteric field of theoretical research into the nature of matter that is far removed from the understanding of most people. Yet, the language by which such theories are expressed can be remarkably common and everyday, including subatomic particles that have been given names such as *quarks, charmed quarks* and *flavored quarks.*

The growth in the blend word's popularity since Carroll's day may also reflect the influence of modern educational trends which have increasingly emphasized scientific and technical training at the expense of classical education. Perhaps, as public education shifted to a more pragmatic curriculum, the corresponding decline in classical language training made inevitable that process by which English has supplanted Greek and Latin as the most accessible source of the raw materials needed to fashion the new words of a modern age.

The following collection of blend words thus serves as yet another example of the impact of science and technology on modern English.

In addition to the obvious role of electronic communications and the mass media in helping to popularize modern slang, major contemporary sources of new words, including the fields of aerospace and military technology, animal and plant hybridization, metallurgy, the advertising industry, the television and movie industries, rock music, and the drug culture are all well-represented in the modern lexicon of the portmanteau word.

With so many aspects of popular culture utilizing the blend word so often, it may even be that the portmanteau word will eventually prove to be as durable as the English language itself.

ABBREVIATIONS

AA	*The Annotated Alice*, Gardner
AEM	*American English*, Marckwardt
AET	*American English*, Tucker
AHD	*American Heritage Dictionary*
AL	*The American Language*, Mencken
AM	*Atlantic Monthly Magazine*
AS	*American Shelter*, Walker
AT	*American Talk*, Hendrickson
BAI	"Blends Are Increasing," Bryant
BAR	*The Barnhart Dictionary of New English (2nd ed.)*
BD	*A Browser's Dictionary*, Ciardi
BDC	*The Barnhart Dictionary Companion*, Barnhart
BDN	*The Barnhart Dictionary of New English (1st ed.)*
BG	*The New American Bartender's Guide*, Poister
BJ	*The Book of Jargon*, Miller
BL	"Blends," Pound
BN	*Brave New Words*, Sherk
BNE	*The 2nd Barnhart Dictionary of New English*, Barnhart
BNW	*The Morrow Book of New Words*, Mager
BPF	*Brewer's Dictionary of Phrase & Fable*, Evans
BTC	*Brands and Their Companies*, Wood
DA	*Doublespeak in America*, Pei
DAS	*Dictionary of American Slang*, Wentworth & Flexner
DCS	*The Dictionary of Contemporary Slang*, Green
DD	*Doublespeak Dictionary*, Lambdin
DED	*Dictionary of Euphemism & Other Doubletalk*, Rawson
DJ	*Newspeak: A Dictionary of Jargon*, Green
DNW	*Dictionary of New Words*, Reifer
DOC	*Dictionary of Computer Data Processing*, Rosenberg
DS	*Dictionary of Slang*, Partridge
DST	*McGraw-Hill Dictionary of Scientific and Technical Terms*

DWP	*Morris Dictionary of Word & Phrase Origins*, Morris
FO	*Food*, Root
FW	*Family Words*, Dickson
HDC	*Harper Dictionary of Contemporary Usage*, Morris
ID	*The Insomniac's Dictionary*, Hellweg
IH	*I Hear America Talking*, Flexner
IPE	*In Praise of English*, Shipley
ISC	*I Stand Corrected*, Safire
JA	*Jargon*, Homer
JD	*Johnson's Dictionary*
JO	*Joy of Lex*, Brandreth
LWW	*The Language of World War II*, Taylor
MBD	*Mrs. Byrne's Dictionary*, Byrne
MBN	*More Brave New Words*, Sherk
MI	*Musical Instruments*, Marcuse
MOT	*Movies on TV*, Scheuer
NA	*Names*, Dickson
ND	*New Dictionary of American Slang*, Chapman
NOL	*Names on the Land*, Stewart
NTC	*NTC's Dictionary of Slang*, Spears
NW	*Longman Guardian New Words*, Mort
NWD	*New Words Dictionary*, Lemay
NWE	*Dictionary of New Words in English*, Berg
OE	*The Oxter English Dictionary*, Saussy
OED	*Oxford English Dictionary*
OL	*On Language*, Safire
OTW	*On the Wisdom of Words*, Wagner
OWW	*Our Own Words*, Dohan
PBW	*The Pears Book of Words*, Brandreth
SB	*The Story Behind the Word*, Freeman
SBD	*A Second Browser's Dictionary*, Ciardi
SE	*The Story of English*, McCrum
SEL	*The Story of the English Language*, Pei
SL	*Slang*, Dickson
SOL	*The Story of Language*, Pei
SSS	*Spoonerisms, Sycophants, & Sops*, Black
STY	*Slang Today and Yesterday*, Partridge
SWW	*Success with Words*
TA	*The Archaicon*, Barlough
TGP	*The Grand Panjandrum*, Hook

TM	*Time Magazine*
TND	*Trade Names Dictionary*, Wood
TW	*The Word*, Laird
VT	"Vocabulary of Time Magazine," Firebaugh
VTR	"Vocabulary of Time Magazine Revisited," Yates
WAW	*Words About Words*, Grambs
WE	*Webster's Third International Dictionary*
WES	*12,000 Words: A Supplement*
WO	*Words*, Dickson
WSC	*Words in Sheep's Clothing*, Pei
WTG	*What's the Good Word?* Safire
WW	*Weasel Words*, Pei
WWA	*Words & Ways of American English*, Pyles
YNW	*500 Years of New Words*, Sherk

Note on Trademarks

The following list of blend words includes a selection of more than 600 distinctive trademarks and brand name portmanteaus. These entries are indicated by capitalizing the initial letter of each brand name, followed by the words *brand name*, a brief description of the product or service, and the name of the manufacturer or parent company. In some circumstances, the use of a specific trademark registration symbol may also be required when certain brand names appear in print. For example, the familiar ® symbol identifies the registered trade name of a product, while ^{SM} may be used to identify the trade name of a service. Anyone intending to include a brand name in a publication is advised to contact the company providing that product or service to determine the specific format required.

Portmanteau Dictionary

A

abhorrible *adj.* (abhor + horrible) Dreadful; detestable. OED

abjective *n.* (abject + objection + adjective) In newspaper jargon, a correction notice appearing in response to a complaint from an injured party. Because of its unrepentant tone, the correction actually does little to satisfy the complainant. JA

abnormous *adj.* (abnormal + enormous) Abnormal or irregular. WE

abortuary *n.* (abortion + mortuary) An abortion clinic, labeled as such by foes of legalized abortion.

Abracurldabra *brand name* Hair-curling appliance, Windmere Corp. BTC

absolete *adj.* (absolute + obsolete) Complete, finished, or done with. Also **obsolute**. OED

abstemperous *adj.* (abstemious + temperate) Moderate in regard to dietary habits. BL

abusak *n.* (abuse + Muzak) A slang term for elevator music. SL

acceleread *vb.* (accelerate + read) The act of increasing one's reading speed, usually referring to the effect of having been enrolled in a speed reading course. MBN

Accorgon *brand name* Accordions, Syn-Cordion Musical Instruments Corp. BTC

Accortina *brand name* Accordion concertinas, Kay Guitar Co. BTC

Accuratone *brand name* Hearing aids and accessories, Telex Corp. BTC

Accuratronic *brand name* Watches, Bulova Corp. BTC

Acrobot *brand name* Child's toy, Tomy Corp. TND

Activision *brand name* Computer software, Mediagenic. BTC

acutangular *adj.* (acute + angular) Having acute angles. OED

adaptitude *n.* (adapt + aptitude) A special ability or aptitude. WE

administralia *n.* (administration + Australia) The upper echelon of corporate management, a realm which is, for many employees, as remote and mysterious as a distant foreign land. JA

administrivia *n.* (administrate + trivia) A derisive name for the presumed duties of an administrator. JO

adrenergic *adj.* (adrenalin + energic) Pertaining to physiological actions and reactions resulting from the release of adrenalin. DNW

Adultrike *brand name* Adult tricycles, Ret Bar Cycle Mfg. Co., Inc. BTC

Advantedge *brand name* Message boards, Marsh Chalkboard Co. BTC

Advertag *brand name* Labels and tags, Denny-Reyburn Co. BTC

adverteasement *n.* (advertisement + tease) Newspaper slang for a phony print ad which is meant to help determine whether customers are actually reading a newspaper's printed advertising. WW

Adverteasing *brand name* Game, Cadaco, Inc. BTC

advertique *n.* (advertisement + antique) An antique collector's name for a piece of early advertising material. OED

advertorial *n.* (advertisement + editorial) A feature in a newspaper or magazine which appears as an editorial, but is paid for by an advertiser. NW

Aerobicycles *brand name* Computerized exercise bicycles, Universal Gym Equipment, Inc. BTC

Aframerican *n.* (African + American) An American of African ancestry. OED

Afrasian *n.* (African + Asian) Of, or belonging to, both Africa and Asia. WE

Africar *n.* (Africa + car) A light all-terrain vehicle which has been designed for use in the African wilderness. NW

Africrafts *brand name* Woodenware figurines, drums, stools, Holladay International. BTC

aggranoy *vb.* (aggravate + annoy) Australian slang, meaning to annoy. DS

aggrovoke *vb.* (aggravate + provoke) Australian slang, meaning to incite or provoke. DS

Agitank *brand name* Photographic developing tank, Yankee Photo Products, Inc. BTC

agreemony *n.* (agree + acrimony) Agreeableness, the opposite of acrimony. OED

agrimation *n.* (agriculture + automation) The use of automated systems in farming. AM

agrindustry *n.* (agriculture + industry) A comprehensive term encompassing the various manufacturing and service industries related to agriculture. BNE

ailevator *n.* (aileron + elevator) An airplane control surface that combines the functions of an aileron and an elevator. Also known as an **elevon**. WE

Airacuda *n.* (air + barracuda) The name given to an American fighter-bomber aircraft introduced in 1937. AEM

airbrasive *adj.* (air + abrasive) Pertaining to the grinding of tooth surfaces with a stream of abrasive particles under air or gas pressure. WE

airdraulic *adj.* (air + hydraulic) Characteristic of a process which combines pneumatic and hydraulic operations. WE

airmada *n.* (air + armada) A large group or formation of warplanes. DAS

airphibian *n.* (air + amphibian) An all-purpose vehicle proposed by futurists during the 1950s. The airphibian was to be an airplane equipped with removable wings and propeller so that it could be converted for use as an automobile. NA

airtillery *n.* (air + artillery) Bombardment consisting of guided missiles or other long-range weapons fired from surface launchers. DNW

Alaskimo *brand name* Sporting goods, Stearns, Mfg. Co. BTC

albertype *n.* (Albert + type) An engraving process for producing multiple prints from a single photographic plate, invented by the German photographer Joseph Albert. DST

alcoholiday *n.* (alcohol + holiday) A holiday in which the primary activity is the drinking of alcoholic beverages. SEL

aldermanity *n.* (alderman + humanity) The quality of being an alderman. DS

alegar *n.* (ale + vinegar) Vinegar made from ale; malt vinegar. WE

alibiography *n.* (alibi + autobiography) An autobiography offered as an explanation or apology for the behavior of the author. WW

Aliencounter *brand name* Computer software, Milliken Publishing Co. BTC

alphabetterment *n.* (alphabet + betterment) Government agencies or programs which are meant to promote economic recovery and social welfare, so-named because they are often characterized by acronymic labels such as HUD or HEW. MBD

alphameric *adj.* (alphabet + numeric) Consisting of both letters and numbers. WE

alphametic *n.* (alphabetic + arithmetic) A mathematical puzzle in which a problem is presented using letters instead of numerals. BDN

altazimuth *n.* (altitude + azimuth) The location of an airplane in flight, as determined by its distance from the ground and its relation to the arc of the curved horizon. ID

altiloquence *n.* (altitude + eloquence) High-flown or pompous oratory. WAW

alundum *n.* (aluminum + corundum) A hard material created by fusing aluminum in a furnace, used mainly as an abrasive agent. OED

Amazone *brand name* Perfume and bath items, Hermark, Inc. BTC

ambiloquence *n.* (ambiguous + eloquence) Skill in the art of double talk. WAW

ambisextrous *adj.* (sex + ambidextrous) A characteristic of one whose sex is not readily distinguishable by appearance alone. Also used to describe a person who is bisexual. WE

Amerasian *n.* (American + Asian) A person of mixed American and Asian ancestry. WES

Amerathon *brand name* Tires, Carlisle Corp. BTC

Amerenglish *n.* (American + English) The particular form of English that is spoken in the United States. OED

Americaid *n.* (America + aid) A word coined by staff members of the Nixon administration in 1972, offered to take the place and also to relieve the stigma of the word *welfare*. WO

Americanecdote *n.* (American + anecdote) An anecdote that involves Americans, or is characteristic of American life. Coined by Clifton Fadiman, it suggests a useful means of classifying anecdotes by nationality, as in Canadianecdotes, Mexicanecdotes, Europeanecdotes, etc.

Americards *brand name* Christmas cards, Americom Corp. TND

Americola *brand name* Soft drinks, Polar Corp. BTC

Americold *brand name* Refrigeration compressors, White Consolidated Industries, Inc. BTC

Americrafts *brand name* Decorative accessories, The Root Candle Co. BTC

Americut *brand name* Steel siding, Alside, Inc. BTC

Amerindian *n.* (American + Indian) An Indian of the North American continent. Amerindian is used to differentiate between a member of the native American tribes and the inhabitants of the Asian subcontinent. AL

ampacity *n.* (ampere + capacity) A means of rating current-carrying capacity as measured in amperes, used primarily to rate the capacity of electrical power cables. DST

ampersand *n.* (and + per se + and) A word which serves as the name for the symbol &. WE

Amplifire *brand name* Heat extractors for fireplaces, Portland Willamette Division of Thomas Industries, Inc. BTC

Ancobar *n.* (Ancona + barred Plymouth Rock) A breed of domestic fowl, developed by crossing Ancona with barred Plymouth Rock chickens. WE

anecdotage *n.* (anecdote + dotage) Advanced age when accompanied by a tendency to reminisce. A person exhibiting such characteristics may be called an **anecdotard.** WE

Angelicare *brand name* Uniforms, Angelica Uniform. BTC

Angelicreation *brand name* Uniforms, Angelica Uniform. BTC

Anglistics *n.* (Anglo + linguistics) The study of the structure and development of the English language. DNW

animatronics *n.* (animal + electronics) Techniques of traditional puppetry combined with modern electronics to create special effects for use in modern film animation. NW

animule *n.* (animal + mule) American frontier slang serving as a means of addressing an obstinate mule, later used in reference to any stubborn or troublesome animal. AET

aniseed *n.* (anise + seed) The seed of anise, an herb commonly used as a flavoring in cordials and cooking. WE

ansurge *n.* (answer + surge) A name given to the sense of being overcome by an irresistible urge to answer the telephone whenever it rings. WO

anticer *n.* (anti + icer) A substance which is used to prevent the formation of ice. OED

anticipointment *n.* (anticipation + disappointment) A sense of great anticipation, immediately followed by great disappointment. Used most often to describe an advertising or broadcasting venture that fails to be as successful or as popular as anticipated. AM

aphidozer *n.* (aphid + hopperdozer) A device consisting of a hopper and revolving brushes, used to brush off and collect aphids from cultivated crops. WE

applaudience *n.* (applaud + audience) An audience determined to be favorable to a performer or performers. An applaudience has every intention of applauding at the conclusion of a performance, regardless of its merit. FW

applaudit *n.* (applaud + plaudit) A vigorous expression of approval. OED

Applessence *brand name* Hair-care products, Brown Drug Co., Inc. BTC

apprehendicitis *n.* (apprehend + appendicitis) Psychiatric jargon, referring to a condition in which intense feelings of apprehension are the cause of acute abdominal pain. SEL

Apricoating *brand name* Fruit icing, Adolph J. Mainzer, Inc. BTC

Aqualarm *brand name* Pool and spa flow switches, boat alarms, Aqualarm, Inc. BTC

archaeolatry *n.* (archaeology + idolatry) Worship of anything ancient or archaic. MBD

arcology *n.* (architecture + ecology) A totally integrated city or environment enclosed within a single structure. Futurists typically envision geodesic domes large enough to encompass entire cities as an essential component of such a system. DJ

argle *vb.* (argue + haggle) To argue in a heated fashion. BL

argufy *vb.* (argue + signify) To argue. An American colloquialism dating from at least the mid–18th century. AET

Ariachne *n.* (Arachne + Ariadne) William Shakespeare's blending of the names of two famous thread bearers of ancient myth. Ariadne provided the thread that helped guide Theseus out of the Minotaur's labyrinth, while Arachne challenged the goddess Athene to a spinning contest, and was transformed into a spider when she lost. The name Ariachne appears in Act V of *Troilus and Cressida;* it's uncertain whether Shakespeare simply confused the two names, or deliberately blended them to accommodate the meter of the passage. IPE

Aristocat *brand name* Toy cat, Elka Toys. BTC

Arithmetickle *brand name* Computer software, Houghton Mifflin Co. BTC

Arkahoma *n.* (Arkansas + Oklahoma) That which combines elements characteristic of the states of Arkansas and Oklahoma. Arkahoma is the name often given to the drawling manner of speech typical among CB radio enthusiasts. TM

armoraider *n.* (armor + raider) Military slang for a soldier assigned to be the crew member of a tank or other armored vehicle. NWE

Aromance *brand name* Aroma disk system, Charles Of The Ritz Group Ltd. BTC

Aromanilla *brand name* Vanilla flavorings, The Aromanilla Co., Inc. TND

Artilleray *brand name* Toy accessory, Mattel, Inc. TND

Artray *brand name* Art supply boxes, Universal Industries. BTC

Asbestile *brand name* Roof flashing and cement, Manville Corp. BTC

asiotic *adj.* (asinine + idiotic) Idiotic; foolish. BL

Asphalastic *brand name* Asphalt paint, Remien & Kuhnert Co. BTC

astrometry *n.* (astronomy + geometry) The branch of astronomy which deals with the geometric relationships of celestial bodies. DST

Athleticare *brand name* Elastic bandages, cold packs, Johnson & Johnson. BTC

Atlashield *brand name* Paints, Atlas Chemical Co. BTC

Atmosphear *brand name* Recording label, Mystic Records. BTC

atomaniac *n.* (atom + maniac) A person who self-righteously proposes using atomic weapons on any country with a political ideology different from his own. DS

atomechanics *n.* (atom + mechanics) The mechanics of atoms; the physical laws that determine the structure and behavior of atomic particles. OED

Atomicronic *brand name* Watches, The Gruen Watch Co. BTC

Atomist *brand name* An electric mist sprayer, RL Corp. BTC

austempering *n.* (austenitic + tempering) A process for heat-treating austenitic steel, an alloy of gamma iron and carbon. DST

austern *adj.* (austere + stern) Of a severe and austere demeanor. Coined by John Wycliffe, 14th century English theologian. BL

Australasian *n.* (Australian + Asian) Consisting of or characterized by a combination of that which is Australian and Asian. OED

Australorp *n.* (Australian + Orpington) An Australian breed of the black Orpington, a species of domestic fowl originally bred in England. DS

autel *n.* (auto + motel) A motel; autel eventually disappeared from common usage because of the public's preference for the word **motel**. DNW

autobesity *n.* (auto + obesity) Advertising jargon coined by automobile dealers to describe an excess of vehicles on their sales lots. DD

automobility *n.* (automobile + mobility) The use of automobiles for transport. WE

autopia *n.* (auto + utopia) A society which is dominated by the automobile. BNW

avigation *n.* (aviation + navigation) The science of aircraft navigation. WE

azaleamum *n.* (azalea + chrysanthemum) Any of the varieties of profusely flowering dwarf chrysanthemum. WE

backini *n.* (back + bikini) A woman's bathing suit that is designed to fully expose the wearer's back. BAI

bacronym *n.* (back + acronym) An acronym in which the word formed by the initial letters appears to have been deliberately chosen to refer back to what is being abbreviated. An example of a bacronym would be SLOSH, a computer simulation used by the National Hurricane Center to determine the potential effects of a hurricane tidal surge, derived from "Sea Lake Overland Surges from Hurricanes." FW

bacterinert *adj.* (bacteria + inert) Resistant to the growth of bacteria. DNW

badvertising *n.* (bad + advertising) Advertising that is offensive, dim-witted or inept. Also, the name of an award given by *Adweek Magazine* acknowledging particularly egregious examples of such advertising. TM

baffound *vb.* (baffle + confound) To baffle or perplex. BL

Bakerloo *n.* (Baker + Waterloo) The name given to a major route in London's underground rail system, running between Waterloo Station and Baker Street. Substituted for the original name of "Baker Street & Waterloo Line," Bakerloo was first suggested by London's *Evening News* newspaper, and officially adopted in 1906. STY

Bakespeare *n.* (Bacon + Shakespeare) A hypothetical historical figure, whimsically proposed as a compromise in the debate regarding whether Sir Francis Bacon is actually the author of Shakespeare's plays. Also: **Shacon.** DS

balloonatic *n.* (balloon + lunatic) Military slang for a person who served in the observation or barrage balloon corps in either world war. DS

ballute *n.* (balloon + parachute) A small inflatable parachute deployed for the purpose of stabilization or deceleration, usually before a conventional chute opens. WES

Baltimorons *n.* (Baltimore + morons) A derogatory name for the residents of Baltimore, Maryland. Coined by journalist Harry Black of the *Baltimore Evening Sun* in 1922. AL

bandstration *n.* (band + orchestration) The scoring of music for a band. WE

banjoey *n.* (banjo + joey) A banjo player. *Joey* is British slang for a clown, derived from the name of Joseph Grimaldi, famous 19th century English comic actor and clown. DS

banjolin *n.* (banjo + mandolin) A musical instrument combining the characteristics of a mandolin and a banjo. OED

banjorine *n.* (banjo + tambourine) A banjo with a short neck, probably so-named because the belly and tension hoop of a banjo resemble a tambourine. WE

banjulele *n.* (banjo + ukulele) A musical instrument which combines the characteristics of a banjo and a ukulele. OED

bardolatry *n.* (bard + idolatry) Adoration of anything having to do with William Shakespeare. MBD

baritenor *n.* (baritone + tenor) A vocalist with the voice of a baritone and the range of a tenor. TGP

barnacular *n.* (barn + vernacular) Another name for government gobbledygook; the use of the word *barn* is a scatological reference to the presumed origin of such material. WAW

barococo *adj.* (baroque + rococo) An architectural or decorative style characterized by grotesquely elaborate features, or by the combination of elements of the baroque and rococo styles. BNW

barsolistor *n.* (barrister + solicitor) British slang for an attorney at law. Barsolistor acknowledges the two distinct types of attorney in Britain, since a barrister is expected to argue cases in court, while a solicitor specializes in out-of-court work. BL

bash *vb.* (bang + smash) To strike with a crushing blow. DS

Basicoat *brand name* Paints and varnishes, Payson Corp. BTC

Bassassin *brand name* Sporting goods, Burke Flexo Products Co. BTC

Basstar *brand name* Guitars and accessories, Modulus Graphite Products. BTC

Basstroker *brand name* Fishing rods, California Tackle Co., Inc. BTC

bastich *n.* (bastard + son of a bitch) An individual whose abrasive personality appears to combine all of the characteristics of a bastard and a son of a bitch. TW

Batheraphy *brand name* Mineral bath salts, General Therapeutics, Inc. TND

Bathinette *brand name* Portable bathtub for infants, Century Products, Inc. BTC

bathtize *vb.* (bath + baptize) To baptize by total immersion. MBN

Batmania *n.* (Batman + mania) The name given to the record-breaking box office popularity of the 1989 movie *Batman.*

Beanimals *brand name* Bean-bag animals, Possum Trot Corp. BTC

Beastro *brand name* Pet products, Bowhaus Designs, Inc. BTC

Beatles *n.* (beat + beetles) The name of a popular British music group, coined in imitation of Buddy Holly's band "The Crickets." The variation in spelling is a punning reference to "beat" music, suggested by Beatle John Lennon.

Beautideal *brand name* Window blinds and fabrics, Steven Fabrics Co. BTC

beautility *n.* (beauty + utility) That which combines the qualities of beauty and utility; design which is as practical as it is beautiful. A person who strives for this aesthetic ideal may be known as a *beautilitarian.* BNE

beefalo *n.* (beef + buffalo) A hybrid of beef cattle and the American buffalo, typically 3/8 buffalo and 5/8 domestic stock. Also: **cattalo.** WES

Beenut Butter *brand name* A blend of peanuts and honey, American Natural Foods, Inc. BTC

beerage *n.* (beer + peerage) A derisive name for the British peerage; any group of English brewers, particularly those who have been made peers. WE

beerocracy *n.* (beer + bureaucracy) Collective term for a group or organization of brewers and tavern owners. DS

beerstro *n.* (beer + bistro) Slang for a tavern. SEL

beezer *n.* (beak + sneezer) A slang name for a person's nose. WE

begincement *n.* (beginning + commencement) A beginning. BL

belkupping *n.* (belch + hiccuping) Belching and hiccuping, occurring simultaneously. BL

bellcony *n.* (bell + balcony) A bell tower. BL

Bellegro *brand name* Clocks, P.B.M. International Corp. TND

belletrist *n.* (belles + lettres) A literary aesthete. SWW

bellygram *n.* (belly + telegram) A variety of telegram in which delivery of the telegram message is accompanied by a belly dancing performance. TM

bellyrina *n.* (belly + ballerina) A belly dancer. BAI

Bestaste *brand name* Canned foods, J. G. Pieri Co., Inc. BTC

Bestemps *brand name* An employment service, Bailey Employment System, Inc. BTC

bestraught *adj.* (beset + distraught) Distressed or overwhelmed by a multitude of woes. BL

Bestyle *brand name* Slippers, Goldberg & Co., Inc. BTC

bewilderness *n.* (bewilder + wilderness) A state of total confusion; a sense of having lost one's bearings or sense of direction; a state of constant tension between sensations of freedom and restraint. TM

biffy *adj.* (bosky + squiffy) In a drunken state. *Bosky* and *squiffy* are British slang words, meaning *drunk*. DS

Bikexpert *brand name* Bicycle parts and accessories, Gallop Cycle. BTC

Bikextras *brand name* Bicycle accessories, Cycle Products Co. BTC

binge *n., vb.* (bung + bilge) A long drinking bout; the act of indulging in such a bout. A bung is the hole drilled through the lower part, or bilge, of a cask. BL

bingle *n.* (bob + shingle) A woman's hairstyle that is characterized by a short bob, partly shingled at the back, also referred to as *bingling*. WE

Binocolors *brand name* Binoculars, Tasco Sales, Inc. BTC

Birdangle *brand name* Bird feeder and toy, Rednour & Smith Mfg. Co., Inc. BTC

Birome *n.* (Bickham + Jerome) A community in Texas, believed to have been named after the two sons of the town's founder. NOL

birthquake *n.* (birth + earthquake) Another name for the "population explosion." DA

biscake *n.* (biscuit + cake) Another name for a biscuit. OED

Bisquick *brand name* Baking mix, General Mills, Inc. BTC

bit *n.* (binary + digit) Computer jargon for an individual piece of data, the smallest part of a binary number. DWP

bitini *n.* (bitsy + bikini) An extremely skimpy woman's two-piece bathing suit. JO

Bitinis *brand name* Women's panties, Munsingwear, Inc. BTC

bitumastic *n.* (bitumen + mastic) A combination of asphalt and filler, used primarily as a coating to protect metals from weathering and corrosion. DST

bizark *adj.* (berserk + bizarre) Strangely frenzied. FW

bizotic *adj.* (bizarre + exotic) That which is odd, strange, or rarely seen. SL

blacketeer *n.* (black market + racketeer) Journalistic slang for a racketeer dealing in the black market. DS

blacksploitation *n.* (black + exploitation) One of a series of relatively low-budget films popular in the 1970s, featuring black characters in stereotypical super-hero roles. Also spelled **blaxsploitation.** DJ

Blacula *n.* (black + Dracula) The title of a 1972 blacksploitation film in which the lead character, a vampire, is black. MOT

bladderdash *n.* (bladder + balderdash) Nonsensical speech or writing. OED

blandiloquence *n.* (bland + grandiloquence) Smooth or flattering speech, intended to soothe emotions instead of arousing them. DS

blandlubber *n.* (bland + landlubber) A person whose diet consists exclusively of bland food. BAI

blandscape *n.* (bland + landscape) Scenery distinguished primarily by the fact that it lacks any interesting features.

blash *vb.* (blaze + flash) To blaze or flare up suddenly. BL

blastard *n.* (blast + bastard) Military slang for a robot bomb, used by the English in World War II to describe Germany's V-1 and V-2 rockets. DNW

blastissimo *adj.* (blast + fortissimo) Very loud, particularly when referring to rock music. ND

bletcherous *adj.* (blech + lecherous) Unpleasant, disgusting and nasty, "blech" being a common interjection made in response to something unpleasant. ND

blort *n.* (blow + snort) Slang term for cocaine, referring to the habit of inhaling it through the nose. DCS

blotch *n.* (blister + botch) An imperfection or blemish. WE

bloterature *n.* (blot + literature) A word coined by John Colet (1467–1519), Dean of St. Paul's Cathedral, to describe written works of "filth and abuse." SEL

blottesque *adj.* (blot + grotesque) Characteristic of a roughly executed painting. OED

bloviate *vb.* (blow + orate) The act of delivering a windy oration, often used to describe a political speech. TGP

blowmobile *n.* (blow + snowmobile) A snow sledge driven by an airplane propeller. WE

bluff *n.* (butch + fluff) Slang for a female homosexual who alternates between active (butch) and passive (fluff) roles. DCS

blunderhead *n*. (blunder + dunderhead) A blundering, muddle-headed person. OED

blunge *vb*. (blend + plunge) A word used in the pottery trade to describe the act of amalgamating or blending; to beat up or mix in water. WE

blunk *n*., *adj*. (blind + drunk) Drug slang for a half-drunk or stuporous condition. DS

blurb *n*. (blurt + burble) A publicity notice, especially one appearing on the dust jacket of a book. Coined in 1907 by American humorist Gelett Burgess, who once defined "to blurb" as "to make a noise like a publisher." BD

blurt *vb*. (blow + spurt) To speak thoughtlessly or impulsively. SB

Boatank *brand name* Marine fuel tanks, Bettcher Mfg. Co. BTC

Boatape *brand name* Electrical tape, Quick-Cable Corp. BTC

boatel *n*. (boat + hotel) A hotel located near water, and equipped with docks to accommodate persons traveling by boat; a cruise ship equipped with all the amenities of a large hotel. WES

bodacious *adj*. (bold + audacious) Complete and unmitigated; extremely bold or brazen. Also spelled **boldacious**. WE

boffo *n*. (box + office) Show business slang for any production that is extremely successful in terms of box office revenue. DWP

boil *n*. (boy + girl) A teenager whose sex is not immediately discernible. DS

bomfog *n*. (bombast + fog) Political bombast that is full of sound and fury, but signifies nothing, and does nothing to clarify any idea or issue. DJ

bomphlet *n*. (bomb + pamphlet) A propaganda leaflet dropped from an airplane. LWW

Bondoggle *n*. (Bond + boondoggle) A motion picture that fails in its attempt to imitate the popular formula of a typical James Bond movie. BAI

bonk *vb.* (bump + conk) To strike or crash into. BAI

boobarian *n.* (boob + barbarian) An habitually crass, stupid or vulgar person. Coined by H. L. Mencken. AL

boobocracy *n.* (boob + bureaucracy) Government by imbeciles. Coined by H. L. Mencken. MBD

booboisie *n.* (boob + bourgeoisie) Coined by Mencken to describe a class of people distinguished mainly by their stupidity and boorishness. AL

booklegger *n.* (book + bootlegger) A smuggler of books. Coined as a means of referring to those persons who managed to smuggle copies of the banned first edition of James Joyce's novel *Ulysses* into the United States. TM

boost *vb.* (boom + hoist) To push or shove from below. WE

bootician *n.* (bootlegger + beautician) Proposed by H. L. Mencken in 1925, at the height of Prohibition, as a means of designating "a high-toned, big-city bootlegger." AL

bootique *n.* (boot + boutique) Advertising slang for a shoestore which specializes in catering to women customers. DD

boozician *n.* (booze + musician) A drunkard. DS

Borotuke *n.* (Bororo + Otuke) A common language stock of the Bororo and Otuke tribes of Brazil and Paraguay. WE

Bosox *n.* (Boston + Sox) A shorthand way of referring to the Boston Red Sox, a professional baseball team.

Bosphorescence *n.* (Bosphorus + phosphorescence) A name given by journalists to the speculative financial investments undertaken by European banks in Turkey during the years 1900–07. The investments were initially promoted as shining opportunities, but they eventually proved to be disastrously unsound for the financiers involved. DS

bouffancy *n.* (bouffant + fancy) An effect of fullness in women's clothing, achieved through the use of voluminous skirts. The word *fancy* appears as a mere accident of spelling, although the implied meaning is appropriate to the style of such attire. WE

bovie *n.* (book + movie) A book based on the screenplay of a movie, and produced in order to capitalize on the movie's popularity. MBN

boylesk *n.* (boy + burlesque) A variety show, particularly one that includes striptease acts and male performers, and intended to appeal to a homosexual audience. DJ

Braford *n.* (Brahman + Hereford) A variety of beef cattle developed by crossing Brahman and Hereford stock. WE

Bralusion *brand name* Foundation garments, Warnaco, Inc. BTC

Brandstand *brand name* Retail shoe stores, United States Shoe Corp. BTC

brandstanding *vb.* (brand [name] + grandstanding) Ambitious promotion of a brand name product. ISC

brangle *n.* (brawl + wrangle) A harsh squabble or dispute. WE

Brangus *n.* (Brahman + Angus) A variety of hybrid beef cattle which is 3/8 Brahman and 5/8 Angus stock. WES

branwagon *n.* (bran + wagon) A word used to describe the food industry's rush to introduce new products containing bran, promoted as an important element in a healthy diet. An example of its use would be the phrase "jumping on the branwagon." NW

brash *adj.* (bold + rash) Prone to act in a headlong or foolhardy fashion; impulsive. WE

bratitude *n.* (brat + attitude) The characteristically stubborn, arrogant, or ill-mannered behavior of adolescents, especially while attending school. Believed to have been coined, appropriately, by a high school principal. DA

Breathingirdle *brand name* Foundation garments, Breathinbra/Slackees, Inc. BTC

Bren *n.* (Brno + Enfield) A light shoulder-fired machine gun, widely used in the British armed forces. Originally manufactured by a weapons firm in Brno, Czechoslovakia, and later produced under special license by the Royal Small Arms Factory in Enfield, England. WE

breviloquence *adj.* (brevity + eloquence) Characterized by brevity in one's speech. WE

Bridallure *brand name* Bridal gowns, Alfred Angelo. BTC

Bridgeasy *brand name* A bridge table cover, E. Errett Smith, Inc. BTC

Briefolio *brand name* Folders, Colad, Inc. BTC

Brilliantone *brand name* Aluminum paint, Zolatone Process, Inc. BTC

Briluminum *brand name* Aluminum paint, Breinig Brothers Corp. TND

brinkles *n.* (bed + wrinkles) Marks left on a person's face by folds or seams in a blanket, sheet or pillow after awakening. FW

Brisbanality *n.* (Brisbane + banality) A derisive name given to the notoriously platitudinous comments of Arthur Brisbane, former editor and columnist for the chain of newspapers owned by William Randolph Hearst. AL

broast *vb.* (broil + roast) A commercial method of cooking that involves deep frying food at higher than ordinary temperatures for a shorter time in order to preserve more of its flavor.

broccoflower *n.* (broccoli + cauliflower) A vegetable that is green like broccoli, but with a compact head of fleshy stalks and buds that is similar to cauliflower.

bromidiom *n.* (bromide + idiom) A commonplace or hackneyed expression. WE

Broncolor *brand name* Photographic equipment, Ehrenreich Photo-Optical Industries, Inc. BTC

Bronzeal *brand name* Door weather strip, Zegers, Inc. BTC

brunch *n.* (breakfast + lunch) A meal combining elements of breakfast and lunch, or served midway between the time when breakfast and lunch are customarily eaten. After it was introduced around 1890, the word became so popular that for a time all blend words were referred to as *brunch words*. YNW

bruncheon *n*. (breakfast + luncheon) A more recent variation of **brunch**, apparently coined because of its snob appeal. SWW

brunner *n*. (breakfast + lunch + dinner) All three meals of the day combined into one ample feast. BN

brustle *vb*. (bustle + rustle) Making a rustling noise while bustling about. OE

brutal nitrate *n*. (brutal + butyl nitrate) The colloquial name given to butyl nitrate, a stimulant containing isobutyl alcohol, also known as "popper" or "poor man's cocaine." BDN

brutalitarian *n*. (brutal + totalitarian) One who advocates or practices physical brutality as an aspect of personal behavior or political doctrine. WE

bubby *n*. (buddy + baby) A slang term of affectionate address, used to refer to an acquaintance of either sex in a fashion similar to "buddy." DCS

bubukle *n*. (bubo + carbuncle) A boil or pimple. A bubo is an inflamed abscess, such as those which signal the onset of bubonic plague. OE

Budgetool *brand name* Trowels, Goldblatt Tool Co. BTC

buffion *n*. (buffoon + ruffian) A buffoon. OED

bugology *n*. (bug + biology) In student slang, another name for biology class. DAS

bulgine *n*. (bull + engine) A steam locomotive. WE

bulimarexia *n*. (bulimia + anorexia) An eating disorder consisting of frequent binging and purging, practiced as a means of sustaining weight loss and controlling appetite. OED

bullionaire *n*. (bullion + billionaire) One who has become wealthy by dealing in the gold market. BAI

bullivant *n*. (bull + elephant) A large, clumsy person. DS

bumbersoll *n*. (bumbershoot + parasol) An umbrella. BL

Bundies *brand name* Panties, Stern-Maid Nitewear, Inc. BTC

bungaloafer *n.* (bungalow + loafer) A person who lounges about in a bungalow. BL

bungersome *adj.* (bungle + cumbersome) Awkward or clumsy. WE

burble *vb.* (burst + bubble) To make a gurgling or bubbling sound. Lewis Carroll once explained that he had fashioned the word by borrowing sounds from *bleat, murmur* and *warble*, but later confessed that he couldn't remember exactly where it had come from. Burble is now commonly used by aerospace engineers to describe the turbulence created when currents of air flow around an object. AA

bureaucrap *n.* (bureaucrat + crap) A derisive name for the official pronouncements of government agencies. WAW

bureaucrazy *n.* (bureaucracy + crazy) Government policy or procedure that is characterized by illogic and confusion. BDN

bureaucrock *n.* (bureaucrat + crock) A pretentious, incompetent government official. BAI

bureausis *n.* (bureaucracy + neurosis) An inability to cope with even the simplest of bureaucratic rules and regulations. WO

burletta *n.* (burlesque + operetta) A short comic opera. MBD

Burnishine *brand name* Metal polishers and cleaners, Burnishine Products, Inc. BTC

buscapade *n.* (bus + escapade) A group tour by bus that is enlivened by a series of improbable events or comic misadventures. TM

butterine *n.* (butter + margarine) A blend of margarine and butter, resulting in a product that is supposed to taste like butter, with less fat and calories. **Butterine** was also the name given to margarine when it was first introduced in England; its use was outlawed in 1887, after farmers objected that the word led the public to mistake margarine for real butter. AL

buttlegger *n.* (bootlegger + butt) A person engaging in the illegal transport or sale of cigarettes upon which no taxes have been paid. BNE

cabarazy *adj.* (cabaret + crazy) A psychological condition characterized by an obsession with nightclubs and the gaudy lifestyle of the cabaret. BL

cabatoe *n.* (cabbage + potato) A hybrid plant which produces a head of cabbage aboveground and potatoes below. WO

cafetorium *n.* (cafeteria + auditorium) A room in a school that is used as both a cafeteria and an auditorium. SEL

Calculighters *brand name* A cigarette lighter, Park Lane Associates, Inc. TND

Calendater *brand name* Calendars, Columbian Art Works, Inc. BTC

Calendial *brand name* Watches, Bulova Corp. BTC

Calexico *n.* (California + Mexico) A city in California located just north of the Mexican border, near Mexicali. NA

Califamous *brand name* Slips, Blou Slip Co., Inc. TND

californicate *vb.* (California + fornicate) The process by which natural landscape is ravaged by uncontrolled urban sprawl, in the manner typical of Southern California. BNE

calligram *n.* (calligraphy + anagram) A visual pun; a word drawn or printed to form a visually arresting picture or image. DJ

Calmanac *brand name* Calendars, Columbian Art Works, Inc. BTC

Calneva *n.* (California + Nevada) A name given to one of three locations on the California-Nevada border where railroads crossed in the mid–19th century. The other two crossing points were known as *Calvada* and *Calada*. NOL

camelcade *n.* (camel + cavalcade) A procession of camels, as in a caravan. AL

camelopard *n.* (camel + leopard) A name the ancient Greeks gave to an African animal that is shaped like a camel, with a spotted hide similar to that of a leopard. The animal was known as a camelopard until the mid–16th century, when it began to be referred to by its modern name of "giraffe." JD

camelry *n.* (camel + cavalry) A contingent of troops mounted on camels. WE

Cameralarm *brand name* Gadget bag with built-in alarm, Spiratone, Inc. TND

camerantics *n.* (camera + antics) Unorthodox activities or behavior involving the use of a camera. Also: *camerabatics*. BAI

camerature *n.* (camera + caricature) A distorted photographic portrait. WO

camouflanguage *n.* (camouflage + language) Language which is intended to deceive, or in some way to disguise the truth. AM

Campoo *brand name* Carpet shampoo and cleaner, Multi-Care Corp. BTC

camporee *n.* (camp + jamboree) A gathering of boy scouts or girl scouts for the purpose of holding contests or exhibitions of scoutcraft. When such an event is held in the winter, it's commonly referred to as a *freezoree*. WE

Campusport *brand name* Sportswear, Campus Sportswear Co. BTC

Canadarm *n.* (Canada + arm) A remote-controlled device which was built in Canada for use on the American space shuttle to manipulate cargo in space. BDC

Canalaska *n.* (Canada + Alaska) The name of a mountain situated on the border of Alaska and Canada. NA

candelabracadabra *n.* (candelabra + abracadabra) Literally, the "magic of candlelight"; the means by which candles are used to create distinctive moods or decorative effects. TM

Candelicious *brand name* Candy, Warner-Lambert Co. BTC

cangle *vb.* (cajole + wrangle) To quarrel or dispute. WE

Canoah *brand name* Canoes, Noah Co. TND

canogganing *n.* (canoe + tobaggoning) A winter sport in which one or more persons slide downhill by riding a canoe instead of a toboggan. WO

canola *n.* (Canada + granola) An alternative name for rapeseed, promoted by an organization of Canadian rapeseed growers in order to avoid the unsavory overtones suggested by the grain's original name. DED

canoodle *vb.* (canoe + paddle) The act of paddling a canoe. BL

Canvaseal *brand name* Canvas waterproofing coating, Everseal Mfg. Co., Inc. BTC

Canvaskin *brand name* Canvas textured paper, Bee Paper Co. BTC

caplet *n.* (capsule + tablet) A coated medicine tablet in the shape of a capsule. BAR

caraburger *n.* (carabao + burger) Ground meat derived from the carabao, a species of water buffalo native to the Philippines. LWW

carbecue *n.* (car + barbecue) A room-sized oven which is designed to melt away the unsalvageable components of an automobile while it revolves on a large spit. OWW

Carboloy *n.* (carbon + alloy) Trademark for a hard metallic substance produced through powder metallurgy, consisting primarily of cemented carbide of tungsten, with cobalt or nickel as a binder. WE

carcinomenclature *n.* (carcinogen + nomenclature) A derisive name for government gobbledygook. The use of **carcinogen** refers to the tendency of bureaucratic language or paperwork to relentlessly multiply, spread and overwhelm. WAW

cargador *n.* (cargo + stevedore) A stevedore assigned to load or unload a ship's cargo. WE

Cargoyle *brand name* Toy vehicles, Mattel, Inc. BTC

carideer *n.* (caribou + reindeer) A hybrid of the caribou and the reindeer. WE

carnibbleous *adj.* (carnivorous + nibble) Carnivorous. BL

carnivoracity *n.* (carnivorous + voracity) An acute appetite for flesh. OED

Carpentree *brand name* Framed pictures and prints, Carpentree, Inc. BTC

Carpetriever *brand name* Vacuum cleaner, Advance Machine Co. BTC

Carroushelf *brand name* Lazy susans, Lescoa, Inc. BTC

Carust *brand name* Automobile rust treatment products, Turtle Wax, Inc. BTC

cascode *n.* (cathode + cascade) A type of grounded cathode tube. OED

Casseiver *brand name* Audio equipment, H. H. Scott, Inc. BTC

cassingle *n.* (cassette + single) A tape cassette consisting of only one or two recorded songs, marketed to take the place of "single" 45 rpm records. BAR

catapunch *n.* (catapult + punch) A spring-activated center punch which can be used to stamp or pierce material without employing a hammer.

catazine *n.* (catalog + magazine) A sales catalog which also features some editorial content. BNW

cattalo *n.* (cattle + buffalo) A meat animal that has been bred in the United States since the 1880s, produced by crossing a female polled Angus with a male American bison. FO

Catviar *brand name* Cat food, Ralston Purina Co. BTC

Cedaroma *brand name* Red-cedar gifts and accessories, Blair Cedar & Novelty Works, Inc. TND

celebutante *n.* (celebrity + debutante) A young woman who becomes a celebrity upon her first appearance in society; someone who seeks the limelight by associating with celebrities. BDC

cellophane *n.* (cellulose + diaphane) Transparent sheets of material composed primarily of cellulose and diaphane, widely used in various types of product packaging. WSC

celtuce *n.* (celery + lettuce) A celery-like vegetable derived from a variety of lettuce, with thick, succulent stems and unpalatable leaves. Also known as "asparagus lettuce," the flavor of celtuce has been compared to either celery or lettuce. WE

Cemestos *n.* (cement + asbestos) Trade name for a wall panel made of fiberboard with asbestos cement facings, used extensively during the post-war building boom in the United States in the construction of prefabricated homes. AS

censcissor *vb.* (censor + scissor) The excising of morally objectionable material from a written work. PBW

Centrahoma *n.* (central + Oklahoma) The name of a city in central Oklahoma. NOL

Centralia *n.* (central + Australia) A name given to the remote central region of the Australian continent. OED

ceramagnet *n.* (ceramic + magnet) A magnet that is a composite of metallic and ceramic materials. DST

ceramal *n.* (ceramic + alloy) A combination of ceramic materials and metal alloys, resulting in a substance noted for its resistance to high temperatures. Also **cermet**. OED

Ceramichrome *brand name* Ceramic products, Ceramichrome, Inc. BTC

Ceramicritters *brand name* Ceramic molds, Duncan Enterprises. BTC

chackle *vb.* (chatter + cackle) A British dialect word, meaning "to cackle or rattle." WE

chaffinch *n.* (chaff + finch) A species of finch, named for its habit of scratching for food among threshed or winnowed husks of grain. OED

chairborne *adj.* (chair + airborne) The status of Air Force officers who were assigned to desk jobs instead of flying combat missions during World War II. LWW

chairoplane *n.* (chair + aeroplane) An amusement park ride consisting of a revolving wheel with seats hanging on chains so that they swing out when the wheel is revolved. WE

Charaids *brand name* Preselected titles for charades, Learning Things, Inc. BTC

Charbray *n.* (Charolais + Brahman) A variety of beef cattle developed in the southern United States by cross-breeding Charolais with Brahman stock. WE

charitarian *n.* (charity + humanitarian) A person who devotes a large amount of time and energy to charitable activities. WE

Charmaid *brand name* Bras and girdles, Charma, Inc. BTC

Charmaternity *brand name* Nursing and maternity bras, Charma, Inc. BTC

Charmour *brand name* Bras and girdles, Charma, Inc. BTC

Chartape *brand name* Tape, Artist Aid. BTC

chastigate *vb.* (chastise + castigate) To correct by rebuke or admonishment. SSS

Cheeslicers *brand name* Cheese slicers, C. J. Schneider Mfg. Co., Inc. BTC

chemagination *n.* (chemistry + imagination) The imaginative use of chemicals in the research and development of new products. BAI

chemiloon *n.* (chemise + pantaloon) A woman's undergarment that resembles a pants slip, advocated as an alternative to rigid stays and corsets by 19th century American physician and feminist Mary Walker. AET BL

chemiluminescence *n.* (chemical + luminescence) The emission of light as the result of a chemical reaction, with no apparent change in temperature. DST

chemonomics *n.* (chemical + economics) The economic aspects of the chemical industry. DNW

chemurgy *n.* (chemistry + metallurgy) A branch of chemistry concerned with the utilization of raw materials in industry. NWE

chessel *n.* (cheese + well or vessel) A large cheese vat. WE

Chessie *n.* (Chesapeake + Nessie) The popular name given to a sea monster believed to live in Chesapeake Bay. The name is patterned after "Nessie," a colloquial name for the Loch Ness Monster. WO

Chewels *brand name* Sugarless liquid-center chewing gum, American Chicle Co. BTC

Chicagorilla *n.* (Chicago + gorilla) A name given to the mobsters who ruled Chicago by means of bribery, intimidation and violence during the Prohibition era. Coined by Walter Winchell. DD

Chicargot *n.* (Chicago + argot) The British term for a style of speech characterized by an overabundance of American slang. DS

chipe *vb.* (cheep + whine) To speak with a high-pitched voice in a persistent, complaining manner. DS

chizzly *adj.* (chilly + drizzly) Uncomfortably wet, cold weather. FW

Choclair *brand name* Chocolate-coconut liqueur, Heublein, Inc. TND

chocoholic *n.* (chocolate + alcoholic) A person addicted to chocolate.

Chocolips *brand name* Chocolate-covered potato chips, U.S. Chocolate. BTC

choff *n.* (chow + scoff) A slang term for food, scoff being slang for the act of eating. DCS

chortle *vb.* (snort + chuckle) To utter a gleeful chuckling or snorting sound. Coined by Lewis Carroll. WE

Chromedge *brand name* Trim for walls, B. & T. Metals Co. BTC

Chromonica *brand name* Harmonicas, H.S.S. Hohner. BTC

Chudge *brand name* Cheese fudge, Original Herkimer County Cheese Co., Inc. TND

chuff *n., vb.* (chug + huff) An irregular sound made by noisy exhaust or exhalations, as in the sound made by a steam engine; the act of making such a sound. WE

chump *n.* (chunk + lump) Literally, a blockhead. WE

Chunnel *n.* (Channel + tunnel) A railroad tunnel beneath the English Channel, linking England with France. First proposed in the 19th century, construction of a Chunnel was opposed by military leaders in both countries, who feared that it could be used as an invasion route. Construction of a modern-day Chunnel began in 1987. DWP

chuppie *n.* (Chicano + yuppie) An upwardly mobile person of Hispanic descent. SL

churchianity *n.* (church + Christianity) Excessive devotion to a particular church. WE

churkey *n.* (chicken + turkey) A hypothetical hybrid resulting from the cross-breeding of a chicken and a turkey. Also known as a "turken." OED

cigaroot *n.* (cigarette + cheroot) A slang word for a cigarette. DAS

cinemactress *n.* (cinema + actress) A movie actress. Normally used when describing an actress appearing exclusively in films, with little or no experience on the stage. A male counterpart is a *cinemactor.* DNW WWA

cinemaddict *n.* (cinema + addict) A person who habitually goes to see motion pictures. DNW

Cinemage *brand name* Movie-film editor, Hudson Photographic Industries, Inc. BTC

cinemagpie *n.* (cinema + magpie) A film actor or actress whose performance is characterized by excessive talk. BAI

cinemalefactor *n.* (cinema + malefactor) A motion picture villain. TM

cinemammoth *n.* (cinema + mammoth) An elaborately produced, extremely expensive motion picture. BAI

cinemaniac *n.* (cinema + maniac) A person obsessed with motion pictures or motion picture celebrities. DNW

cinemenace *n.* (cinema + menace) A movie villain. BAI

cinemogul *n.* (cinema + mogul) A powerful person in the movie industry, particularly a producer at a major movie studio. NWE

Cinnamint *brand name* Chewing gum, Clark Gum Co. BTC

circannual *adj.* (circa + annual) Characterized by or appearing in yearly cycles or periods. WES

citrange *n.* (citrus + orange) A hybrid variety of orange, produced by cross-breeding a hardy trifoliate orange with a common sweet orange. The result is a highly aromatic fruit, somewhat bitter to the taste. FO

citrangequat *n.* (citrange + kumquat) A citrus fruit which is the hybrid of a citrange and a kumquat, resulting in a small, acidic, limelike fruit. WE

Citruslim *brand name* An appetite suppressant, Source Naturals. TND

cittern *n.* (cither + gittern) A guitar with a pear-shaped body and wire strings, popular in Renaissance England. **Cither** and **gittern** are names for similar stringed instruments of that period. WE

clacket *vb.* (clack + racket) To "clack" or make noise like a hen; to chatter. OED

Clamato *brand name* Clam and tomato juice, Motts USA. BTC

clamburger *n.* (clam + hamburger) A hamburger patty containing ground or chopped clams. AL

Clampipe *brand name* Electrical supplies, Mueller Electric Co. BTC

clantastical *adj.* (clandestine + fantastical) Pertaining to a hidden or imaginary phenomenon. BL

clash *vb.* (clap + crash) To collide or strike together with a loud noise; to conflict or disagree. WE

Classicrepe *brand name* Crepe paper, Cindus Corp. BTC

Classicurl *brand name* Hair-curling irons, Ming Dynasty, Inc. BTC

clavicylinder *n.* (clavichord + cylinder) A friction bar instrument in the shape of a square piano, invented in 1799. Clavicylinder music is produced by depressing keys on a keyboard, causing bars of graduated lengths to press against a wet glass cylinder rotated by a foot treadle. MI

claviola *n.* (clavichord + viola) A keyboard instrument in the shape of an upright piano, featuring metal strings sounded by a continuous bow. MI

Cleanamel *brand name* Enamel cleaner, J.N.T. Mfg. Co., Inc. BTC

clevertivity *n.* (clever + creativity) A tendency to be creative in a clever sort of way.

Climatest *brand name* Paints, Pioneer Paint & Varnish Co. BTC

Climatube *brand name* Pipe insulation, Nomaco, Inc. BTC

climatype *n.* (climate + type) A variety of plant or animal life which occurs as a distinct species because of the effects of climate or other environmental factors. WE

clinicar *n.* (clinic + car) A vehicle specially equipped and staffed to provide medical treatment in remote areas. DNW

Clipad *brand name* Clipboards, Elbe-Cesco, Inc. BTC

cloof *n.* (cloven + hoof) A cleft, cloven hoof. WE

clump *n.* (chunk + lump) A lump or mass. WE

clunch *vb.* (clench + clutch) To clench or grasp tightly. OED

coastel *n.* (coast + hotel) A barge or floating barracks equipped with sleeping accommodations and moored near a coast to provide convenient off-shore lodgings. BDC

Coca-Colonialism *n.* (Coca-Cola + colonialism) Incorporation of American commercial product and trademark names into a foreign language. SE

cockapoo *n.* (cocker spaniel + poodle) A hybrid of the cocker spaniel and poodle. WES

cocomat *n.* (coconut + mat) Matting made of coconut fiber. WE

Cointainer *brand name* Coin holders and wrappers, Data-Link Corp. BTC

colaholic *n.* (cola + alcoholic) A person addicted to cola drinks. ND

Colorail *brand name* Handrail moldings, Julius Blum & Co., Inc. BTC

Coloray *brand name* Pencils, Faber-Castell Corp. BTC

Colorinse *brand name* Hair-care products, The Neslemur Co. BTC

coloroto *n.* (color + roto) A rotogravure image that is printed in more than one color. WE

Combots *brand name* Computer game, The Avalon Hill Game Co. BTC

Combrush *brand name* Comb and brush, Solo Products Corp. BTC

Comfitables *brand name* Men's underwear, Hanes Hosiery. BTC

Commart *n.* (Common + mart) An economic association formed among western European nations, more often referred to as the "Common Market." BAI

commershills n. (commercial + shills) Personal appearances by celebrities in television commercials, selling products the celebrities may or may not actually use. WW

Communicards *brand name* Language materials, Communication Skill Builders, Inc. BTC

Communicenter *brand name* Intercom/telephone answering system, Nutone. BTC

communiversity *n.* (commune + university) A university organized and managed according to the egalitarian standards of a commune. OWW

commyrot *n.* (commie + tommyrot) A derisive name for communist ideology or propaganda. DA

compander *n.* (compressor + expander) A device which compresses transmission signals as they are sent, and also expands them upon reception. BNE

compossible *adj.* (compatible + possible) A social or political condition in which coexistence between opposing groups is possible. An arrangement of this kind may not represent complete harmony, but it does at least allow a measure of tolerance among the parties involved. TGP

compregnate *vb.* (compress + impregnate) To use heat in compressing thin sheets of wood impregnated with resins or chemical compounds into a dense, hard substance. WE

compunications *n.* (computer + communications) A communications system operated by or dependent upon computers. BDC

compushency *n.* (compulsion + push + urgency) An extreme sense of urgency. BL

computeracy *n.* (computer + literacy) Knowledge of or experience with computers; the state of being "computerate." OED

Computeradio *brand name* Housewares, General Electric Co. BTC

Computrainers *brand name* Bicycling trainers, Racer-Mate, Inc. BTC

Comradar *brand name* Personal communications products, Comradar Corp. BTC

comrogue *n.* (comrade + rogue) A companion in roguery. BL

conceptacle *n.* (conception + receptacle) Any body cavity shaped like a flask, with a pore opening to the outside, and containing reproductive structures. DST

conclusory *adj.* (conclusion + illusory) A decision, opinion or judgment which appears to be based on facts, but actually is not. FW

concubub *n.* (concubine + bub) A slang term utilizing "bub," an informal form of male address, to create a masculine variation of the word "concubine." Concubub is used to designate the male half of a couple living together out of wedlock. WW

Condenstop *brand name* Pipe-coating spray, Utility Mfg. BTC

condomarinium *n.* (condominium + marina) A condominium complex where the residents are provided access to a boat marina. Also: **boatel.** DA

condorminium *n.* (condor + condominium) The popular name given to a specially designed aviary at the San Diego Wild Animal Park, where rare California condors are cared for and bred. TM

condotel *n.* (condo + hotel) A hotel offering suites for purchase under terms similar to those of a condominium.

confectionate *adj.* (confection + affectionate) Sweetly affectionate. FW

congloperator *n.* (conglomerate + operator) A derisive name given to the chief executive of a multinational corporation when that person is distinguished by his lack of competence. Also known as a **consloperator.** TGP

Containeramp *brand name* A mobile loading ramp, JH Industries, Inc. BTC

Contemprints *brand name* Paper accessories, Contemprints. BTC

contraption *n.* (contrivance + trap + invention) A popular slang term for any complicated device. WE

Controlock *brand name* Security products, Silent Watchman Corp. BTC

Conturedge *brand name* Copper foil tape for glass art, Lamps Ltd. BTC

copelessness *n.* (cope + hopelessness) A psychological condition characterized by a sense of helplessness and an inability to cope with life. DNW

Corduct *brand name* Cord protectors, The Wiremold Co. BTC

Cornfetti *brand name* Popcorn, National Oats Co., Inc. BTC

Corntillas *brand name* Corn torillas, Garden of Eatin'. BTC

cornucopious *adj.* (cornucopia + copious) Abundant. OED

corpocracy *n.* (corporate + bureaucracy) The bureaucratic structure of a large business or corporation. BDC

Correctext *brand name* Computer software, Houghton Mifflin Co. BTC

correctify *vb.* (correct + rectify) To correct. OED

correctitude *n.* (correct + rectitude) Correctness of behavior, especially in regard to formal rules of etiquette. TGP

corrupie *n.* (corrupt + yuppie) An ambitious yuppie who would abandon any standard of moral behavior to achieve success. NW

Cosmedicake *brand name* Medicated makeup, Kay Preparation Co., Inc. BTC

Cosmerica *brand name* Makeup, Cosmerica, Inc. BTC

cosmoceutical *n.* (cosmetic + pharmaceutical) A cosmetic prescribed by doctors to help improve the health and appearance of a patient's skin. NWD

Costumakers *brand name* Craft products, Blumenthal & Co., Inc. BTC

costumary *adj.* (costume + customary) Of or belonging to a costume. OED

coulometer *n.* (coulomb + meter) Another name for a voltameter, a device for measuring the amount of electricity passing through a conductor. WE

Counterange *brand name* Smooth-top ranges and ovens, Amana Refrigeration, Inc. BTC

cowbot *n.* (cow + robot) A robot which is designed to feed and milk a herd of dairy cows. AM

Craftint *brand name* Art supplies, Vogart Crafts Corp. BTC

Craftip *brand name* Pen sets, Bio-Pak Associates. BTC

craisin *n.* (cranberry + raisin) A cranberry which has been dried and sweetened for use in breakfast cereals, or as a snack food.

cramble *vb.* (crawl + amble) An English dialect word, meaning to walk or move stiffly, or with difficulty. WE

crant *n.* (cover + grant) A government grant awarded to a private group under a fake project title so that the money can eventually be used as funding for covert intelligence operations. JA

Crantastic *brand name* Cranberry juice drink, Ocean Spray Cranberries, Inc. BTC

crawk *n.* (croak + squawk) Radio slang, used to designate the person assigned to imitate animal sounds on the air. MBD

Crawligator *brand name* An infant's toy, Creative Playthings. BTC

Creamassage *brand name* Body rub, Stanlabs Pharmaceuticals Co. BTC

Creamedic *brand name* Antiseptic soap, Harley Chemicals. BTC

Creativeyes *brand name* Optical products, Caesar, Inc. BTC

cremains *n.* (cremate + remains) Human ashes; the residue that is left after a cremation. WE

cricketiquette *n.* (cricket + etiquette) Traditional rules of conduct regulating behavior while attending or participating in a cricket match. TM

crinch *vb.* (crimp + pinch) A slang word for the act of bending or denting. DCS

Crinkelastic *brand name* Knit goods, Jantzen, Inc. BTC

Criticare *brand name* Nutritional supplement, Bristol-Myers U.S. TND

Criticolor *brand name* Daylight lamps, Philips Lighting Co. BTC

criticular *adj.* (critical + particular) Selective; discriminating. BL

croissandwich *n.* (croissant + sandwich) A sandwich made by stuffing slices of meat or other filling into a croissant.

croodle *vb.* (crouch + cuddle) The act of hugging in a loving embrace. WO

Crosstich *brand name* Glassware, Owens-Philips Lighting Co. BTC

crough *n.* (crest + trough) A point midway between the crest and the trough of a wave. MBN

crowl *vb.* (croak + growl) To rumble or make sounds in one's stomach or bowel. OED

cruical *adj.* (crucial + critical) Crucial; critical. BL

cruisine *n.* (cruise + cuisine) The food served to passengers on a cruise ship.

Crunchips *brand name* Snack food, Pepsico, Inc. BTC

Crystalace *brand name* Tile, Wenzel Tile Co. BTC

Cubalaya *n.* (Cuba + Malaya) A breed of fowl of Cuban origin which has been crossbred with oriental varieties. WE

cubangle *n.* (cube + angle) The solid angle of a cube, formed by three edges meeting at right angles. OED

cultivar *n.* (cultivated + variety) An organism resulting from cultivation; a cultivated variety. WE

curfloozie *n.* (curfew + floozie) A young woman of dubious morals who exploited the wartime curfew established in American cities in 1945, ordering the closing of all places of entertainment at midnight. The "lively social interaction" which would occur when thousands of women and servicemen were put out into the street at the same time was acknowledged by this coinage in the *New York Daily News*. LWW

Curvedge *brand name* Auto buffing pads, M & H Laboratories. BTC

curvessence *n.* (curve + essence) An advertising coinage describing the flattering feminine curves which are supposed to result from the wearing of a particular garment. BAI

cybot *n.* (cybernetic + robot) A robot capable of making its own decisions by imitating processes of rational thought. SL

Cypresside *brand name* Exterior hardboard siding, Masonite Corp. BTC

daffynition *n.* (daffy + definition) A silly or humorous definition of a word or phrase. WWA

daiquirita *n.* (daiquiri + margarita) A daiquiri made with tequila instead of rum.

Dakoming *n.* (Dakota + Wyoming) The region encompassing either side of the state line between Wyoming and South Dakota, including the Black Hills. AL

dancercise *n.* (dance + exercise) A form of conditioning exercise involving rhythmic dancing to music, usually performed in a group. NWD

dandle *vb.* (dangle + fondle) The act of tossing a child up and down in affectionate play. WE

dang *vb.* (damn + hang) A popular euphemism for *damn*. DS

dastardice *n.* (dastard + cowardice) Cowardice. Coined by English novelist Samuel Richardson. BL

datamation *n.* (data + automation) The technology of automated data storage, retrieval and transfer. JA

dawk *n.* (dove + hawk) A blend word popular during the Vietnam War, when it was used to describe persons who would not take a position either supporting or opposing the war. BNW

debutantrum *n.* (debutante + tantrum) An outburst of bad temper by a young woman in fashionable society. FW

debutramp *n.* (debutante + tramp) A young woman who seeks social status through promiscuous behavior. Coined by Walter Winchell. WW

decathlete *n.* (decathlon + athlete) An athlete who competes in the decathlon. WES

deceleron *n.* (decelerate + aileron) A movable surface mounted on the wing of an airplane, combining the functions of an aileron and an air brake in controlling the plane's speed. WE

Decoraids *brand name* Decorations, Coronet Merchandise Corp. BTC

decoreographer *n.* (decor + choreographer) The person responsible for designing or positioning scenery on a theatrical stage. DNW

decrassify *vb.* (declassify + crass) The editing of crude or objectionable material from publications such as news releases or transcripts prior to their release. TGP

Defendamins *brand name* Vitamins, Nature's Way Products, Inc. BTC

Defendears *brand name* Hearing protection equipment, Weston Laboratories, Inc. BTC

deformeter *n.* (deformation + meter) An instrument for measuring minute deformations in structural materials. WE

Delegance *brand name* Footware, Omni Skates Corp. BTC

Delicare *brand name* Cold-water detergent, Beecham, Inc. BTC

Delicaseas *brand name* Prepared seafood entrees, Kiban Products International, Inc. BTC

Delkaria *n.* (Delhi + Karachi) An alternative name for the Indo-Pakistani subcontinent, derived from the names of the cities of New Delhi, the capital of India, and Karachi, the former capital of Pakistan. DNW

delushious *adj.* (delicious + luscious) Pertaining to something that is remarkably delicious in taste. DS

Democracity *n.* (democracy + city) A hypothetical planned city of the future, portrayed in an elaborate scale model enhanced by background film projection and music, and featured in the United States exhibition at the New York World's Fair in 1939.

democrapic *adj.* (democratic + crap) Pertaining to a form of political hypocrisy, in which a leader expresses earnest support for democratic principles, and yet demonstrates a complete lack of tolerance for those same principles the moment they are perceived as a threat to his political dominance. WO

demonagerie *n.* (demon + menagerie) A diverse gathering of demons. OED

Dependabolt *brand name* Anchor bolts, ITW Ramset/Red Head. BTC

depicture *vb.* (depict + picture) To depict; to imagine. WE

derbish *n.* (debris + rubbish) The unsalvageable remains of a demolished building; rubble. BAI

dermabrasion *n.* (dermal + abrasion) Removal of surface layers of skin by means of an abrasive rotary tool. OED

Dermassage *brand name* Medicated skin cream, Colgate-Palmolive Co. BTC

Deskretary *brand name* Desk calendars, Ad-A-Day Co., Inc. BTC

detectifiction *n.* (detective + fiction) Fiction dealing with the activities of criminals and criminal investigators. TM

diesohol *n.* (diesel + alcohol) A mixture of diesel oil and ethyl alcohol, used as fuel in diesel engines. BAR

Digitime *brand name* Digital recording device, Stancil Corp. BTC

Digitone *brand name* Telephone sets, Northern Telecom, Inc. BTC

Diminuendo *brand name* Foundation garments, Goddess Bra. BTC

Dinersaurs *brand name* Breakfast cereal, Ralston Purina Co. BTC

dingle *n.* (divorced + single) A person who has again become eligible for marriage because of a divorce, dingle being considered a more polite form of address than the term "divorced." WW

dingot *n.* (ding + ingot) A massive lump of metal formed as the result of volcanic activity. DST

Dinosnores *brand name* Stuffed animals, Commonwealth Toy & Novelty Co., Inc. TND

diplonomics *n.* (diplomacy + economics) The use of economic policies to achieve diplomatic goals. JO

dipsy *adj.* (tipsy + dippy) Exhibiting unsteadiness or foolish behavior as the result of having had too much to drink, with a suggestion of the word *dipsomaniac*. SOL

disastrophe *n.* (disaster + catastrophe) A disaster of catastrophic proportions. BL

Discabinet *brand name* Record cabinets, Wallach & Associates, Inc. BTC

Disclean *brand name* Disc-drive cleaning system, Discwasher, Inc. BTC

Discolor *brand name* Recording label, Kubaney Publishing Corp. BTC

Dishtergent *brand name* Dishwashing detergent, Harley Chemicals. BTC

ditsy *adj.* (dizzy + dotty) Lacking seriousness or sensibility. ND

Dixican *n.* (Dixie + Republican) A member of the Republican Party from one of the southern states. BNW

Dixiecrats *n.* (Dixie + Democrats) One of a group of southern Democrats who abandoned the Democratic Pary when it chose to advocate civil rights legislation during the presidential campaign of 1948. WE

Documate *brand name* Filing system, Wright Line, Inc. BTC

docutainment *n.* (documentary + entertainment) A television program presenting factual information in a dramatic or theatrical manner. BDC

doddle *vb.* (dodder + toddle) To move about in a doddering or toddling fashion. WE

doff *vb.* (don + off) The act of removing one's hat or clothing. WE

Dogloo *brand name* Pet shelters, Igloo Dog Homes. BTC

doitrified *adj.* (doited + petrified) Dazed to the point of immobility. Doited is a Scottish dialect word, meaning *confused*. WE

dolfan *n.* (Dolphin + fan) A fan of the Miami Dolphins football team.

Domebrella *brand name* Umbrellas, Domebrella. BTC

Domesticare *brand name* Home-cleaning franchise, Domesticare, Inc. BTC

don *vb.* (do + on) The act of putting on a garment. WO

donkophant *n.* (donkey + elephant) A name coined by political cartoonists to describe an animal which is a cross between a donkey, representing the Democratic Party, and an elephant, the symbol of the Republican Party. In 1911, when the word was first used, the two parties held positions that were virtually the same regarding many national issues. BL

dooby *n.* (dowdy + booby) Australian slang for a person who is hopelessly out of touch or old-fashioned. DS

do-pas-so *n.* (do-si-do + pass) A variation of the standard do-si-do figure in square dancing. WE

dorgi *n.* (dachshund + corgi) The offspring of a dachshund and a corgi. FW

dormantory *n.* (dormant + dormitory) A place where bodies are kept in cold storage; a morgue.

Dorsian *n.* (Dorset + Persian) A hybrid of the Dorset Horn and Persian sheep. WE

doubleton *n.* (double + singleton) In card games such as whist or bridge, when two cards of one suit are in a player's hand. OED

draggle *vb.* (drag + straggle) To trail on the ground; to straggle behind. WE

Drainzyme *brand name* Bacteria booster, Jancyn Mfg. Corp. BTC

dramassassin *n.* (drama + assassin) A theater critic notorious for a tendency to write harshly critical reviews. BAI

dramedy *n.* (drama + comedy) A film, play or television production combining the elements of a drama and a comedy.

dreariment *n.* (dreary + merriment) A dreary or dismal condition. OED

Dresserobe *brand name* Juvenile furniture, Hedstrom Corp. BTC

dresshirt *n.* (dress + shirt) A shirt meant to be worn on formal occasions. BAI

dripple *vb.* (drip + dribble) To dribble briskly. WE

Dripride *brand name* Incontinence products, Dripride. BTC

drismal *adj.* (drizzle + dismal) Pertaining to an extended period of rainy weather, so relentlessly gloomy that it becomes psychologically debilitating. TGP

drizzerable *adj.* (drizzling + miserable) A characteristic of weather that is unpleasantly damp and uncomfortable. Also: **drizzable.** DS

droob *n.* (drip + boob) Australian slang, used to describe an extremely dull person. DS

droppie *n.* (dropout + yuppie) A yuppie who drops out of the competition of professional life to seek an alternative lifestyle. NW

drunch *n.* (drinks + lunch) A lunch consisting mostly of alcoholic drinks, a coinage attributed to Tallulah Bankhead. SOL

Druriolanus *n.* (Drury + Coriolanus) A theatrical nickname for the Drury Lane Theatre in London, with reference to Shakespeare's play *Coriolanus.* DS

Drynamite *brand name* Sump pumps, Goulds Pumps, Inc. BTC

Dualastic *brand name* Elastic hosiery, Bell-Horn. BTC

Dualift *brand name* Bras, Lovable Co. BTC

Duaload *brand name* Tires, The Firestone Tire & Rubber Co. BTC

Ductape *brand name* Pressure-sensitive tape, Arno Adhesive Tapes, Inc. TND

Dulcitar *brand name* Stringed instruments, Ledfords Musical Instruments. BTC

dumbfound *vb.* (dumb + confound) To strike dumb; to amaze. WE

dumfusion *n.* (dumb + confusion) A state of confused stupidity. OE

dunch *vb., n.* (dinner + lunch) The practice of eating a complete dinner at lunchtime; an afternoon meal which functions as both lunch and dinner. DS

dungalow *n.* (dung + bungalow) A derisive name for the functional but nondescript California bungalow, a word used primarily by Southern California real estate developers who demolished many such modest homes during the building boom of the 1980s to make way for sprawling luxury estates. TM

duologue *n.* (duo + monologue) A lengthy conversation between two persons. OED

Durablend *brand name* Sleepwear and lingerie, Henson Kickernick, Inc. BTC

Dustroyer *brand name* Dust mops, American Textile Products Co. BTC

dwizzened *adj.* (dwindle + wizzened) Extremely wrinkled; shrunken by age. BL

Dyenamite *brand name* Fabric dyes, Carnival Arts, Inc. BTC

dynamotor *n.* (dynamo + motor) A motor that performs as both a motor and a generator. WE

earjerker *n.* (ear + tearjerker) A motion picture that prominently features a soundtrack calculated to elicit an emotional response from the audience. DCS

Earthoon *n.* (earth + moon) One of the names proposed for the primordial body which existed during the formation of our solar system, and later broke apart to form the earth and moon. Suggested by physicist George Gamow, who also offered the name *Moorth* as an alternative. BAI

Eastralia *n.* (Eastern + Australia) An Australian name for the eastern region of Australia. DS

echosultant *n.* (echo + consultant) A consultant hired for the express purpose of reconfirming and thus sanctioning the findings of a previous consultant, a ploy often used by government or business officials to justify their own policies. JA

econometric *adj.* (economic + metric) Having to do with the application of mathematical forms and statistical techniques to economic theories and problems. WE

Economiser *brand name* Toilets, Crane Plumbing / Fiat Products. BTC

Economixer *brand name* Gas and lubricant metering devices, OMC Parts & Accessories. BTC

ecotage *n.* (ecology + sabotage) Environmental terrorism; sabotage committed in the belief that acts such as driving spikes into tree trunks to ruin the saws of loggers will help save the environment. NWD

ecotecture *n.* (ecological + architecture) A work of architecture designed specifically to blend into the landscape and harmonize with its natural surroundings. JO

ecstatician *n.* (statistician + ecstatic) A specialist in the art of achieving ecstasy; a sex therapist. DD

ecumaniac *n.* (ecumenical + maniac) A zealous supporter of the ecumenical movement. OED

ecumenopolis *n.* (ecumenical + metropolis) The basis of a theory that envisions all societies of the world evolving into one vast interlocking community, encompassing all nations and cultures in one universal city. TW

edifice complex *n.* (edifice + Oedipus complex) An overwhelming obsession with large, imposing buildings, particularly buildings erected as government offices. DJ

educant *n.* (education + cant) A derisive name for teaching jargon. WAW

Educare *n.* (education + care) An educational program intended for persons at least 65 years old. BAI

educatalog *n.* (education + catalog) A product catalog that also features informative editorial content.

educrat *n.* (education + bureaucrat) An educational bureaucrat. BNW

Effectone *brand name* Metal and wood undercoats, Jones-Blair Co. BTC

Eggcessories *brand name* Easter-egg decorating kits, Imagineering, Inc. BTC

Eggsact *brand name* Egg lecithin, Source Naturals. BTC

Eggspert *brand name* Housewares, J & J Mfg. Corp. BTC

Eggstendables *brand name* Egg products, Schneider Brothers, Inc. BTC

Eggstra *brand name* Canned foods, Tillie Lewis Foods, Inc. BTC

Elasticap *brand name* Roof-paper adhesive, Missouri Paint & Varnish Co. BTC

Elasticlad *brand name* Wall coatings, Missouri Paint & Varnish Co. BTC

elastration *n.* (elastic + castration) Bloodless castration, achieved by fitting a strong rubber band around the scrotum. Elastration is a technique utilized mainly in the breeding of livestock. WE

electionomics *n.* (election + economics) The costs involved in running an election campaign. TM

Electrecord *brand name* Recording label, Worldtone Music, Inc. BTC

electret *n.* (electricity + magnet) A dielectric body in which a permanent state of electric polarization has been achieved. WE

Electricord *brand name* Extension cords, Pacific Electricord Co. BTC

Electrocities *brand name* Electronic jewelry and belts, Electrocities Co. BTC

electrocute *vb.* (electric + execute) The act of killing a criminal by administering a fatal charge of electricity; any act of killing by means of an electrical charge. Coined in 1890 to describe the function of the newly invented electric chair. WWA

electrolier *n.* (electric + chandelier) A chandelier in which electric bulbs have taken the place of candles. AL

electromatic *adj.* (electric + automatic) Pertaining to any electrical equipment that can be operated automatically. OED

electropult *n.* (electric + catapult) An electrical propulsion device that is used to help aircraft accelerate and take off from short runways. DNW

elevon *n.* (elevator + aileron) An airplane control surface that combines the functions of an elevator and aileron. WE

Elmonica *n.* (Eleanor + Monica) The name of a community in Oregon, said to have been named after the daughters of the city's founder. NOL

Elvisitor *n.* (Elvis + visitor) A tourist who visits Graceland Mansion in Memphis, Tennessee, the former home of popular singer Elvis Presley. TM

embargaining *vb.* (embargo + bargaining) The imposing of special conditions upon a journalist by a news source, in which the journalist is given exclusive information with the understanding that it won't be released until permission to do so has been granted by the source. JA

Embracelette *brand name* Watches, Benrus Watch Co. BTC

embrangle *vb.* (embroil + entangle) The act of confusing or involving another in some difficulty. ND

Emersonthusiast *n.* (Emerson + enthusiast) One who is extremely fond of the works of Ralph Waldo Emerson. AL

enduct *n.* (end + product) The final result of a particular project. JA

Energenius *brand name* Thermostats, Jameson Home Products, Inc. BTC

Entergy *brand name* Steel door systems, Ceco Corp. TND

entremanure *n.* (entrepreneur + manure) An enterprise involving an experimental commercial power plant which burns dried cattle chips for fuel. The prototype for such a plant began producing electric power near El Centro, California, in 1988. TM

entreporneur *n.* (entrepreneur + porn) A person engaged in the production or distribution of pornographic materials. BAI

entrepreneurtia *n.* (entrepreneur + inertia) The condition afflicting a corporation when its executive managers, having exerted sufficient effort to reach the top, discourage any similar efforts from lower management personnel that might threaten their own position. DJ

Envelock *brand name* Envelope fasteners, Ames Safety Envelope Co. BTC

Envelopener *brand name* Envelope openers, Omatron Corp. BTC

Enviromelt *brand name* Chemicals for melting ice and snow, Para Products. BTC

Enviromins *brand name* Vitamins, Twin Laboratories. BTC

environics *n.* (environment + electronics) The use of electronic equipment to control environmental conditions, pertaining primarily to the regulation of laboratory environments. BNW

environmental illness *n.* (environmental + mental illness) A chronic inability to regard the environment as anything but an expendable resource to be exploited for profit.

epicurate *n.* (epicure + curate) A clergyman distinguished by his acute fondness for good food. BL

epigrammar *n.* (epigram + grammar) Written or spoken language that is rich in epigrams. TM

epoxidation *n.* (epoxy + oxidation) A chemical reaction yielding an epoxy compound. DST

eroduction *n.* (erotic + production) A film, television program or stage play featuring erotic scenes or episodes. DA

Erusticator *brand name* Rust remover, Albatross USA, Inc. BTC

estatescape *n.* (estate + escape) An estate used as a refuge or vacation retreat. NW

eunanch *n.* (eunuch + anchor) A print journalist's derisive name for a television news anchorperson. JA

euphemantics *n.* (euphemistic + semantics) The business of selling products or services by means of indirect promotional messages. JA

euphobia *n.* (euphoria + phobia) An obsessive fear of good news, generally used in a humorous or satiric sense. BNE

Eurafrican *n.* (European + African) The name given to a race of dark-skinned people who once inhabited both the European and African coasts of the Mediterranean Sea. OED

Eurasian *n.* (European + Asian) A person of mixed European and Asian descent. WE

Eurocracy *n.* (European + bureaucracy) The administrative apparatus of the European Economic Community, or Common Market. BNW

Europhoria *n.* (Europe + euphoria) An attitude of heightened optimism in regard to Europe's future, based on the continent's powerful economic expansion in the '80s and the prospect of increased cooperation among Common Market members. TM

Europort *n.* (Europe + port) A European seaport serving major international markets, and especially trade among the Common Market countries. BAR

Eurosclerosis *n.* (Europe + arteriosclerosis) Europe's economic affliction during the 1970s, characterized by a constricted flow of business activity because of overregulation, underinvestment and waning competitiveness. TM

Eveready *brand name* Flashlights and batteries, Eveready Battery Co. BTC

evidentually *adj.* (evident + eventually) Pertaining to something which is not now apparent, but which will be eventually. FW

exaccurate *adj.* (exact + accurate) Painstakingly precise. PBW

examnesia *n.* (exam + amnesia) The sudden loss of memory often experienced by students while writing an exam. YNW

Excelerator *brand name* Toy vehicle, Mattel, Inc. BTC

Excelight *brand name* Ladders, White Metal Rolling & Stamping Corp. BTC

exclosure *n.* (exclude + enclosure) An area from which animals are excluded by fencing or other barriers. DNW

Executary *brand name* Dictating equipment, IBM Corporate Headquarters. BTC

Exercycle *brand name* Exercise equipment, Exercycle Corp. BTC

expectacle *n.* (expect + spectacle) An event which is awaited with great anticipation. MBN

experieak *n.* (experimental + freak) Computer jargon for a person obsessed with the idea of instant sensory gratification. JA

explaterate *vb.* (explain + elaborate) American slang, meaning to explain further. OWW

expugn *vb.* (expunge + impugn) To expunge or erase; to impugn, or call into question. BL

expunctuation *n.* (expunction + punctuation) The deletion of material from written copy during the process of editing. OED

Exquisiteyes *brand name* Optical products, Caesar, Inc. BTC

extencisor *n.* (extensor + exerciser) A mechanical device designed to aid in exercising and strengthening the fingers and wrist. BNE

Extenzyme *brand name* Contact-lens cleaner, Allergan, Inc. BTC

extrality *n.* (extra + territoriality) The right of jurisdiction claimed by a country in regard to its citizens while they are in another country; a compressed form of the word "extraterritoriality." OED

extreamline *vb.* (extreme + streamline) The process of designing or producing something with a singularly streamlined form.

Fabricadabra *brand name* Bras, Exquisite Form Industries. BTC

Fabricork *brand name* Vinyl plastic bulletin boards, Claridge Products & Equipment, Inc. BTC

Fabricushion *brand name* Stamp pads, Consolidated Business Products. BTC

Fabulace *brand name* Pantyhose, Burlington Industries, Inc. BTC

Fabulash *brand name* Eye makeup, Revlon, Inc. BTC

facho *adj.* (female + macho) An exaggerated sense of female pride, coined by Clare Boothe Luce in answer to the popular use of **macho**. OL

faction *n.* (fact + fiction) A written work that is based on factual material, but written in the style of a fictional novel. BNE

factrip *n.* (fact + trip) A political fact-finding trip, undertaken to gather information about a particular problem or issue. JA

faddict *n.* (fad + addict) A person who tends to compulsively indulge in a fashion or craze. Also: **faddiction.** BDC

fadical *n.* (fad + radical) Someone attracted to a movement or cause simply because it is in vogue, and not because of any real sense of commitment. JA

fagtory *n.* (fag + factory) A manufacturing plant where cigarettes are produced. FW

fakelore *n.* (fake + folklore) Pseudo-folklore presented as genuine and traditional lore, despite the fact that it originates from sources other than folk tradition or belief. Coined by American folklorist Richard Dorson in 1950. WES

fandangled *adj.* (fandango + new-fangled) Of the newest or most novel fashion. DS

fanglomerate *n.* (fan + conglomerate) A kind of rock consisting of fragments deposited in an alluvial fan and consolidated into a single mass. OED

fantabulous *adj.* (fantastic + fabulous) Sublime; extraordinary. DCS

fantigue *n.* (fantastic + fatigue) A state of great excitement or tension. WE

Farmaster *brand name* Fence and gates, Behlen Mfg. Co. BTC

farmerceutical *n.* (farmer + pharmaceutical) Any one of a number of growth hormones used by farmers to increase the growth rate of livestock. NW

Fastamp *brand name* Self-inking stamps, Artistic Greetings, Inc. BTC

Fastart *brand name* Rowing shells and sculls, Peinert Boatworks. BTC

Fasteeth *brand name* Denture adhesive, Vicks Toiletry Products. BTC

Fastoast *brand name* Toasters, The Black & Decker Corp. BTC

Fastrack *brand name* Sliding door hardware, Stanley Hardware Division of Stanley Works. BTC

Fastrength *brand name* Nail-care products, American Cosmetic Mfg. Laboratories, Inc. BTC

Fastroke *brand name* Artist's brushes, Andrew-Mack & Son Brush Co. BTC

Fathometer *brand name* Depth sounders, Raytheon Marine Co. TND

fatiloquent *adj.* (fate + eloquent) Eloquently prophetic. WE

feebility *n.* (feeble + debility) A state of acute physical weakness. PBW

feep *n.* (feeble + beep) The soft beeping sound a computer terminal makes when it is switched on. SL

feevee *n.* (fee + TV) An optional service available to cable subscribers in which more television channels are provided if the subscriber pays an additional monthly fee. BJ

felsic *adj.* (feldspar + silica) Pertaining to a group of light-colored minerals, including feldspar and quartz. OED

femagoguery *n.* (female + demagoguery) An appeal to the basic emotions and fears of women, especially when in regard to economic or political issues. BDC

Femarines *n.* (female + Marines) Military slang for the Women's Reserve of the U.S. Marine Corps during World War II. LWW

femcee *n.* (female + emcee) A female master of ceremonies. DD

feminar *n.* (female + seminar) A presentation or series of presentations intended for an audience of women. JO

femlin *n.* (female + gremlin) Australian slang for what is known in America as a "beach bunny," a young woman who hangs around surfers, but rarely surfs herself. A *gremlin* is a surfing enthusiast who is not very adept at the sport. DS

Fencextender *brand name* Adapters for wood fences, Extol International, Inc. BTC

ferrod *n.* (ferrite + rod) A ferrite rod that is used as a sensing device in computer data files. DOC

fertigation *n.* (fertilization + irrigation) A form of irrigation in which precise amounts of water and nutrients drip onto growing plants. TM

Fictionary *brand name* Board game, Mayfair Games, Inc. BTC

Fidelitone *brand name* Audio equipment and accessories, Fidelitone, Inc. BTC

figitated *adj.* (fidget + agitated) Uneasy; agitated. BL

Filamerican *n.* (Filipino + American) A Filipino who exhibits sympathetic or loyal feelings toward Americans. WE

Filmaker *brand name* Filmstrip maker, Radmar, Inc. BTC

filmosque *n.* (film + mosque) A movie theater designed in the extravagantly arabesque style popular during the 1920s. DA

Finedge *brand name* Glassware, Libby Division of Owens-Illinois, Inc. BTC

finickerty *adj.* (finicky + persnickety) Exhibiting extremely meticulous or exacting standards. DS

Finisheen *brand name* Hair care products, Revlon, Inc. BTC

finitiative *n.* (finish + initiative) The ability to finish what one has started. MBN

Fintastic *brand name* Fish food and aquarium supplies, Fintastic. TND

Fireresist *brand name* Household fabrics, Glen Raven Mills, Inc. BTC

Firmesh *brand name* Outdoor furniture, Ever-Ready Appliance Mfg. Co. BTC

fizzician *n.* (fizz + physician) A soda jerk. Coined by H. L. Mencken. DD

flabbergast *vb.* (flap + aghast) To overwhelm with shock or surprise. DS

flabbergasterisk *n.* (flabbergast + asterisk) A punctuation mark suggested by journalists to serve as a more intense version of the exclamation point. A flabbergasterisk is represented by an exclamation point in which the period is replaced by an asterisk. OTW

flamdoodle *n.* (flam + flapdoodle) Exaggerated, boastful speech; pretentious nonsense. WE

flaperon *n.* (flap + aileron) A control surface mounted on a rocket or guided missile which provides the altitude control of ailerons and the lifting and braking effect of flaps. DNW

Flaprotect *brand name* Card holders, Angler's Co., Ltd. BTC

flare *n.* (flame + glare) A brief, bright flame or light. WE

flarp *adj.* (flat + sharp) In music, a performance that is quavering, tentative or off-pitch. ND

flaunt *vb.* (flout + vaunt) To display vainly and brazenly, in a manner intended to attract attention. SEL

Flavorama *brand name* Barbecue sauces, Flavorite Laboratories, Inc. TND

flavorite *n., adj.* (flavor + favorite) Advertising coinage that is used to designate a preferred food, flavor or taste.

flavory *adj.* (flavor + savory) Rich in flavor. WE

fleep *n.* (fly + jeep) A variety of ultra-light aircraft featuring flexible wings and a small engine, designed for use in rugged areas. BAI

flether *vb.* (flatter + blether) To fawn and flatter. WE

Flexerciser *brand name* Exercise equipment, Saitama Kako Co. BTC

Flexibolts *brand name* Nylon bolts, Heartwood Furniture. BTC

Flextender *brand name* Picture frame hangers, Art-Phyl Creations. BTC

flightseeing *n., vb.* (flight + sightseeing) The viewing of scenic landscapes from the air by means of an airplane or helicopter instead of from a vantage point on the ground.

Flightube *brand name* A kite, The Kite Factory. BTC

flimmer *vb.* (flicker + glimmer) To faintly flicker. OE

flisk *vb.* (flick + whisk) To make a motion of flicking or whisking about, as an animal does with its tail. WE

floatel *n.* (float + hotel) A semi-submersible oil drilling platform fully equipped with living quarters for the workers on board. Also used to describe a cruise ship. AL

flop *vb., n.* (flap + drop) To throw oneself about or down; a failure. WE

Florala *n.* (Florida + Alabama) The name of a community on the border of Florida and Alabama. NA

Floralace *brand name* Knit goods, Jantzen, Inc. BTC

flounder *vb.* (founder + blunder) To proceed clumsily or self-consciously. WE

flounge *n.* (flounder + plunge) The act of plunging into or floundering in a mire. BL

Flozenges *brand name* Fluoride lozenges, Cooper Laboratories. BTC

fluidram *n.* (fluid + dram) A unit of liquid capacity equal to 1/8 of a fluid ounce, often used as an apothecary measure. WE

flump *vb.* (flop + thump) To fall or set down suddenly and violently. DS

flunk *vb.* (flinch + funk) To fail. WE

fluorod *n.* (fluorescent + rod) A rod made of phosphate glass that absorbs ultraviolet light and emits orange fluorescent light. DST

flurry *n.* (flutter + hurry) A sudden, brief rush of wind or fall of snow; a sudden commotion or agitation. WE

flush *vb.* (flash + gush) To flow and spread rapidly; to wash or empty out with a sudden flow of water. WE

flusticate *vb.* (fluster + complicate) To confuse. DS

flustrate *vb.* (fluster + frustrate) To make or become nervous and confused. Also spelled **flusterate**. DS

flycycle *n.* (fly + bicycle) An aircraft powered entirely by muscle-power, utilizing the pedal mechanism of a bicycle to turn the aircraft's propeller. MBN

Foamaster *brand name* Bedding products, Sleepmaster Products Co., Inc. BTC

Foamats *brand name* Foam-rubber place mats, Inventex Corp. BTC

Foldoor *brand name* Folding doors and partitions, Holcomb & Hoke Mfg. Co., Inc. BTC

foolosopher *n.* (fool + philosopher) A shallow or foolish person who pretends to practice philosophy. DS

Footrue *brand name* Shoes, Classic Mold Shoe Co. BTC

foozle *n., vb.* (fool + fizzle) Sports slang for failure to strike what one is attempting to hit; the act of missing or failing during the performance of any sports activity. DS

foozly *adj.* (foolish + woozy) Exhibiting silly or foolish behavior, especially when the result of having had too much to drink. SOL

foppy *n.* (fogey + hippy) One who decides to drop out of conventional society at a relatively advanced age. NW

fozzle *n.* (fog + drizzle) Weather conditions characterized by fog and light rain. Also spelled **foggle**. SOL

frabjous *adj.* (fair + joyous) Joyful; happy. Coined by Lewis Carroll. OED

Franglais *n.* (France + Anglais) Popular French words or phrases which have been borrowed or adopted from English. Examples include *le babysitter, le bluejeans,* and *baseballeur.* SE

fratority *n.* (fraternity + sorority) Student housing open to the emancipated of either sex. The first fratority was founded at a Kansas university in 1913, and intended to provide housing for married couples attending the school. Also known as a **frarority** *or* **sorernity.** DA BL

Frenglish *n.* (French + English) English which is characterized by the frequent use of French words or phrases. BNE

frickles *n.* (fried + pickles) Fried pickles, a snack food popular in the southern United States. SL

frizzle *vb.* (fry + sizzle) To fry something until it is crisp and curled. WE

frontenis *n.* (fronton + tennis) A game of Mexican origin that is played with rackets and a rubber ball on a three-walled court. A **fronton** is an jai alai court. WES

Frostar *brand name* Frozen yogurt, J & J Snack Foods Corp. BTC

Frostea *brand name* Tea mix, Thomas J. Lipton, Inc. BTC

Frostop *brand name* Fast-food franchise, Frostop Corp. BTC

frowzled *adj.* (frowzy + tousled) Disheveled or unkempt. WE

fruice *n.* (fruit + juice) A non-alcoholic fruit drink which can be served at social functions as a substitute for punch. BL

Fruitreats *brand name* Snack food, United Brands, Inc. BTC

frumious *adj.* (fuming + furious) Bad-tempered; violent. Coined by Lewis Carroll. AA

frustraneous *adj.* (frustrate + extraneous) Futile or useless. MBD

fuelish *adj.* (fuel + foolish) Carelessness in the use of gasoline or heating fuel, a word often used in public service announcements admonishing the public to conserve non-renewable energy resources. BNE

fugly *adj.* (fat + ugly) Fat and ugly. NTC

fumorist *n.* (female + humorist) A female humorist or comedian, particularly one who specializes in feminist humor. Also: **fumerist**.

Funbrella *brand name* Children's umbrella, Playskool, Inc. BTC

funch *n.* (fuck + lunch) Slang term for a sexual liaison which has been arranged during one's lunch hour. Also known more politely as a "matinee." DCS

Funcils *brand name* Writing products, Alliance Rubber Co. BTC

funginert *adj.* (fungi + inert) Capable of resisting the growth of fungus, a characteristic similar to *bacterinert.* DNW

Fungiside *brand name* Paints, PPG Industries. BTC

fustle *vb.* (fuss + bustle) To exhibit a state of restless activity or agitation. WE

fusty *adj.* (fungus + musty) Stale or smelly; pertaining to an outdated or old-fashioned person. TGP

futilitarian *n.* (futility + utilitarian) A person who engages in hopelessly futile pursuits. WE

fuzzstache *n.* (fuzz + mustache) A scant wisp of hair on the upper lip of a young man who has not yet begun to shave. BN

fuzzword *n.* (fuzzy + buzzword) A deliberately confusing or imprecise term. OED

galimony *n.* (gal + alimony) Payment in lieu of alimony between estranged lesbians. BNW

galumph *vb.* (gallop + triumph) To march exultantly with irregular, bounding movements. Coined by Lewis Carroll. AA

galvanneal *vb.* (galvanize + anneal) To coat with an alloy of iron or steel and zinc, a process achieved by heating a surface already galvanized with zinc. WE

gamblous *adj.* (gamble + hazardous) Exhibiting a tendency to engage in high-stakes gambling or other forms of risk-taking. DS

gamorous *adj.* (gams + glamorous) Descriptive of a female celebrity famous for her shapely legs, or "gams." SEL

Garbagger *brand name* Leaf-bag holder, Morval-Durofoam Ltd. TND

garbarge *n.* (garbage + barge) A barge loaded with garbage. Garbarge was coined during the summer of 1987 to describe a barge filled with garbage which left New York City and was subsequently turned away from numerous ports of entry.

garbitrageur *n.* (garbage + arbitrageur) A financial speculator who attempts to manipulate the value of stock by spreading rumors and misinformation. SL

garlion *n.* (garlic + onion) A hybrid vegetable, a pungent cross between the garlic plant and the onion. WE

Gasentry *brand name* Hardware, Pelco Industries. BTC

gasid *adj.* (gas + acid) Advertising coinage describing an upset stomach, as in *gasid indigestion.* JO

gasohol *n.* (gasoline + alcohol) Fuel which is a blend of 10 percent ethanol alcohol and 90 percent gasoline.

gasolier *n.* (gas + chandelier) A chandelier equipped with gas jets instead of candles. WE

gaspirator *n.* (gas + respirator) Another name for a gas mask, including a pun on the word "gasp." DS

gastronomer *n.* (gastronomy + astronomer) A lover of fine food; a glutton. OED

gawkward *adj.* (gawk + awkward) Clumsy or stupid. PBW

gayola *n.* (gay + payola) Slang for the practice of paying off police officers to look the other way regarding the activities of gay clubs and bars. DCS

geep *n.* (goat + sheep) The hybrid offspring of a goat and a sheep. BNW

Geometricks *brand name* Hairstyling appliances, Conair Corp. BTC

geriatrickster *n.* (geriatric + trickster) An elderly person who exhibits an impish sense of humor and a fondness for practical jokes. DA

gerrymander *n.* (Gerry + salamander) Redrawing of election districts to give one political party an unfair advantage over the other. Coined in response to the convoluted boundaries resulting from the reapportionment of Essex County, Massachusetts, in 1812 by governor Elbridge Gerry, gerrymander was inspired by a political cartoon depicting the district as a contorted salamander. WE

Giantarts *brand name* Candy, Sunline Brands. BTC

Gidget *n.* (girl + midget) The name of the main character in a series of teen-oriented films, beginning with the original Gidget in a 1959 movie of the same name starring Sandra Dee in the title role. WO

Giftwist *brand name* Chenille twist-on gift ties, Lois April Ltd. BTC

gimble *vb.* (gambol + nimble) To frolic nimbly. Coined by Lewis Carroll. STY

gimp *n.* (game + limp) A lame person. OED

Gingeraffe *brand name* Stuffed toy, KinderGund. BTC

gingerine *n.* (gin + tangerine) A cocktail made from gin, grapefruit juice and tangerine juice. BG

ginormous *adj.* (gigantic + enormous) Extremely large. DD

giraffish *adj.* (giraffe + raffish) Exhibiting a carefree attitude and a tendency to act in a flamboyant manner. WE

girlesque *n.* (girl + burlesque) A burlesque act featuring young women. Coined by Walter Winchell. WAW

giverous *adj.* (give + generous) Generous. BL

Glamarble *brand name* Simulated marble, Dimensional Plastics Corp. TND

glamazon *n.* (glamour + Amazon) A statuesque woman, particularly a well-proportioned movie actress. SEL

Glamirror *brand name* Makeup mirror, Lynch-Jamentz Co. TND

Glassheen *brand name* Concentrated detergent, Advance Chemical Co., Inc. BTC

glassivation *n.* (glass + passivation) A process of making passive (reducing the reactivity) of silicon conductors by encapsulating them in glass. DST

Glidraulic *brand name* Door closers, Illinois Lock Co. BTC

glime *n.* (glaze + rime) A thin coating of ice with a consistency between that of glaze and rime. DST

gliterary *adj.* (glitter + literary) Indicative of a literary style that is pretentious or self-promoting in tone. TM

glitterati *n.* (glitter + literati) A social class composed of the wealthy and the celebrated, made conspicuous by the amount of publicity they receive in the popular press. DCS

glitzy *adj.* (glamorous + ritzy) Ostentatiously glamorous. DCS

glob *n.* (globe + blob) A small drop, globule, smear, or splash. WE

Global Releaf *n.* (relief + re-leaf) The name of a campaign by the American Forestry Association to restore the world's forests as a means of reducing the effects of global warming.

globaloney *n.* (global + baloney) An unrealistic theory or program that is to be implemented on a global scale. Coined by U. S. Representative Clare Boothe Luce in 1942, describing Vice President Henry Wallace's grandiose aid proposal promising to "deliver a bottle of milk on the doorstep of every Hottentot." WSC

glop *n.* (goo + slop) Any gooey, viscous substance. DS

Gloppets *brand name* Glove puppets, Animal Fair, Inc. BTC

Glorifried *brand name* Potato products, Potato Service, Inc. BTC

gloriole *n.* (glory + aureole) In religious art, the depiction of a halo or nimbus around the head or body of a sacred person. WE

Glovely *brand name* Hand cream, Elbee Sales. BTC

glowboy *n.* (glow + cowboy) A nuclear plant worker who is frequently exposed to high levels of radiation for short periods of time. Like his cowboy namesake, a glowboy tends to travel from one job site to another, performing manual work as a temporary, transient employee. AM

glumpish *adj.* (glum + lumpish) Sulky or gloomy. BL

glumpy *adj.* (gloomy + grumpy) Morosely irritable. Coined by novelist Compton Mackenzie. FW

glunch *adj.* (glum + clunch) Moody; sullen. **Clunch** is an English dialect word, meaning *lump*. TA

goditorium *n.* (god + auditorium) A church. MBD

Goldwaterloo *n.* (Goldwater + Waterloo) The 1964 American presidential election, in which Republican candidate Barry Goldwater suffered a devastating defeat. SEL

golfelt *n.* (golf + felt) A type of green felt carpeting, often used as a playing surface at miniature golf courses and artificial putting greens. BAI

gollywog *n.* (golly + pollywog) A black-faced, grotesquely dressed doll with a large shock of fuzzy hair, a popular toy among English children around the turn of the century. OED

gonocide *n.* (gonad + suicide) Surgery to achieve sterilization when performed upon the male sex partner; a vasectomy. DA

Goofix *brand name* Error-correction tape, American Coated Products. TND

goon *n.* (gorilla + baboon) A person hired to intimidate others by means of violence or the threat of violence; a thug. **Goon** originated as the name of a subhuman creature appearing in a cartoon strip by American cartoonist E. C. Segar in the 1930s. NWE

goop *n., vb.* (goo + drip) The dripping of any thick substance onto a surface; any thick, messy substance. WE

gormagon *n.* (gorgon + dragon) A mythical beast with the body of a dragon and the head of a gorgon, a mythical woman-creature with snakes instead of hair; the name of an 18th century English secret society, an offshoot of the Masons. DS

gorp *n.* (gulp + snort) A snack food, also known as trail mix, composed of nuts, raisins, candy and grain. The blend of **gulp** and **snort** has been suggested by William Safire as an alternative to the popular belief that gorp actually stands for "good old raisins and peanuts." SL

Grammy *n.* (gramophone + Emmy) An honorary statuette awarded annually for outstanding achievements in the recording industry. WE

grandacious *adj.* (grand + gracious) Grand in stature, and highly dignified in appearance. AET

grandificent *adj.* (grand + magnificent) Marked by splendor and magnificence. AL

Graphicube *brand name* Frame for photos, Graphicana Corp. BTC

graser *n.* (gamma rays + laser) A hypothetical laser device that would generate radiation in the form of gamma rays. DST

grasple *vb.* (grasp + grapple) To grapple. OED

graunch *vb.* (grate + crunch) To make a grating, grinding or crunching sound. OED

Greatings *brand name* Recipe greeting cards, Hello Studio, Inc. BTC

gribble *vb.* (graze + nibble) To lightly forage on herbage, a word often used to describe the feeding habits of sheep in pasture. DS

grice *n.* (grime + ice) The dense mass of dirt, ice and packed snow that accumulates inside the wheel wells of motor vehicles in wintertime. FW

gridlock *n.* (grid + deadlock) A traffic jam in which a grid of intersecting streets becomes so hopelessly congested that nothing is able to move in any direction. WES

Grinvitations *brand name* Announcements and invitations, Riback Enterprises, Inc. BTC.

gription *n.* (grip + traction) Adhesive friction; traction. FW

grismal *adj.* (grim + dismal) Exceedingly gloomy and miserable. WSC

gritch *vb.* (gripe + bitch) To nag or complain bitterly. DCS

groceteria *n.* (grocery + cafeteria) A grocery store where customers serve themselves and pay for their groceries as they leave. OED

grooly *adj.* (gruesome + grisly) Sinister; nasty. DS

gropple *vb.* (grapple + grope) To grope or come to grips with. OED

groupuscule *n.* (group + minuscule) A very small or inconsequential group. BAR

growsy *adj.* (grumpy + drowsy) Displaying the ill-humored demeanor of someone just awakened abruptly from a deep sleep. DA

grozzle *vb.* (grub + guzzle) The act of greedily consuming food and drink. DS

grubble *vb.* (grub + grabble) To feel or search about uncertainly with one's hands; the act of groping. WE

grum *adj.* (grim + glum) Morose, glum or surly. WE

grumble *vb.* (growl + rumble) To mutter or complain in a surly fashion. SB

gubbish *n.* (garbage + rubbish) Incorrect or useless computer data. SL

guck *n.* (goo + muck) An unpleasant or offensive substance. WE

guestage *n.* (guest + hostage) A guest of a foreign country who is not allowed to leave; a hostage. Coined after the Iraqi invasion of Kuwait to describe the status of foreign nationals forcibly detained by the Iraqi government.

guestimate *n.* (guess + estimate) An estimate made with little or no supporting information; an estimate based equally on guesswork and reasoning. Coined by Lewis Carroll. Also spelled **guesstimate.** WE

Guestray *brand name* Melanine ashtrays, C. P. Plastic Engineering Co., Inc. BTC

Guitarmonize *brand name* Musical instrument polish, American Showster Guitars. BTC

gumbacco *n.* (gum + tobacco) An unsavory combination of chewing gum and tobacco, popular among professional baseball players. FW

gummixed *vb.* (gummed + bollixed) As in *gummixed up*, meaning confused, muddled or ruined. ND

gungineer *n.* (gun + engineer) Military slang for an engineer responsible for the task of mounting heavy guns. DS

gunk *n.* (gunge + junk) Any filthy, sticky or greasy matter; anything objectionably messy or smelly. WE

guppie *n.* (guppy + yuppie) A yuppie active in supporting ecological issues. NW

gustard *n.* (goose + bustard) An archaic name for the bustard, a game bird similar to a crane. BL

gusterly *adj.* (gusty + blustery) Weather conditions characterized by strong, gusty winds. FW

guttle *vb.* (gut + guzzle) To eat voraciously. OED

guzunder *n.* (goes + under) A chamberpot, so-called because it "guz-under" the bed. DS

Gymboree *brand name* Play equipment, The Gymboree Corp. BTC

gyrene *n.* (GI + Marine) A colloquial name for a United States Marine. DAS

Habitank *brand name* Aquariums, Undersea Habitats. BTC

Habitrail *brand name* Small-animal houses, food and accessories, Metaframe Corp. BTC

habitude *n.* (habit + attitude) A particular, habitual way of doing things. TGP

hain *n.* (hail + rain) Precipitation consisting of a mixture of hail and rain. TGP

Hairobics *brand name* Hair-care products, Hairobics. BTC

halfhazardly *adj.* (half-hearted + haphazardly) Lacking in planning, direction, or resolve.

Halternate *brand name* Foundation garments and lingerie, Blue Bay, Inc. BTC

hamateur *n.* (ham + amateur) An actor who compensates for inexperience by overacting. SOL

Hambassador *brand name* Hams, Agar Food Products Co. BTC

Handip *brand name* Detergent, Britex Corp. BTC

handraulic *adj.* (hand + hydraulic) Any process or operation performed by hand instead of by mechanical means. OED

handtector *n.* (hand + detector) A hand-held metal detector similar to those used at security checkpoints in airports. BAR

hangarage *n.* (hangar + garage) A hangar that provides shelter for aircraft. OED

happenstance *n.* (happen + circumstance) A circumstance regarded as being due to chance. Also **happenstantial**. WE

haranag *vb.* (harangue + nag) To scold in a haranguing fashion. Coined by poet and novelist Stephen Vincent Benet. FW

harmolodic *n.* (harmonic + melodic) A style of modern music featuring extensive improvisation and utilizing a variety of keys, tempos and contrasting instruments. BDC

harmonicello *n.* (harmonic + cello) A bowed musical instrument, similar to the viola, utilizing five gut and ten metal strings. MI

harumphrodite *n.* (harumph + hermaphrodite) British slang for a hermaphrodite, *harumph* being a common interjection implying disapproval. OED

Hashbury *n.* (Haight + Ashbury) A colloquial name for the Haight-Ashbury district of San Francisco, a popular haven of the drug culture during the 1960s, including an obvious reference to the word "hash," which is slang for the drug hashish. DAS

hassle *n.* (haggle + tussle) A heated argument. WE

Hawcubites *n.* (Mohawks + Jacobites) A notorious band of ruffians who roamed the nighttime streets of 18th century London. The Hawcubites and the *Mohocks,* another infamous street gang of that era, sought to embellish their reputations for savagery by naming themselves after a North American Indian tribe renowned for the ferocity of its warriors. BPF

haylage *n.* (hay + silage) Partially dried hay that has been stored as livestock forage. WE

Hearphone *brand name* Audio devices, Technical Exhibits Corp. BTC

heartistic *adj.* (heart + artistic) Characteristic of art that dwells on overtly emotional or sentimental themes. PBW

heatronic *adj.* (heat + electronic) Heated by means of an insulated electric current. DNW

hective *adj.* (hectic + active) Feverishly active; agitated. FW

hellennium *n.* (hell + millennium) A thousand-year period in hell, the antithesis of the Christian belief that the second coming of Christ will initiate His thousand-year reign on earth. AL

hellion *n.* (hell + hallion) A disorderly or troublesome person, **hallion** being an archaic word meaning *scamp* or *scoundrel.* WE

hellophone *n.* (hello + telephone) A telephone. BL

hempire *n.* (hemp + empire) A derisive name for the British Commonwealth of Nations, an organization made up mainly of small tropical nations, representing the last remnants of what was once a vast empire. DS

Herbacue *brand name* Food dips, House of Herbs, Inc. BTC

Herblock *n.* (Herbert + Block) Pen name of Herbert Lawrence Block, Pulitzer Prize–winning political cartoonist for the *Washington Post.* WSC

heredipity *n.* (heredity + serendipity) A search of ancestral records in an effort to establish family ties that would legitimize the right to claim a legacy. MBD

herodynamics *n.* (hero + aerodynamics) A hypothetical group of laws governing the fortunes of heroic figures, similar to the natural laws that govern the movements of physical matter, such as "Every epic action has an equal and opposite reaction." TM

herohotic *adj.* (hero + hot + erotic) A euphemism describing the genre of sexually suggestive novels that enjoyed wide popularity around the turn of the century. DS

heroicomic *adj.* (heroic + comic) Relating to comedic material that is ludicrously noble or elevated in tone. WE

hermaphrodite *n.* (Hermes + Aphrodite) An individual possessing both male and female reproductive organs, a word first applied to the androgynous offspring of Hermes and Aphrodite. WE

herstory *n.* (her + history) History written from the female point of view. BDC

hesh *pron.* (he + she) A gender-neutral pronoun, proposed for use in place of either *he* or *she* by H. L. Mencken in 1927. AL

hesiflation *n.* (hesitation + inflation) A period of halting, sporadic economic growth, coupled with high inflation. BNE

hican *n.* (hickory + pecan) The hybrid of a hickory and a pecan tree, the result being a tree that thrives and produces edible nuts in regions farther north than the normal range of the pecan. FO

himmicane *n.* (him + hurricane) A humorous reference to the U. S. Weather Bureau's revised policy of giving hurricanes male names on an alternating basis with females. Before this "de-gendering" policy was adopted in 1979, it was traditional for only female names to be used. During the policy review leading up to the change, it was suggested that the names of certain Congressmen might be even more appropriate for designating dangerous windstorms. BNE

Hinglish *n.* (Hindi + English) Hindi words or phrases borrowed from the English language. HDC

hintimation *n.* (hint + intimation) A slight or indirect indication. FW

hir *pron.* (him + her) A genderless pronoun, proposed for use in place of *him* or *her.*

hirm *pron.* (him + her) A gender-neutral pronoun that may be used in place of either *him* or *her.* WO

hobohemia *n.* (hobo + Bohemia) A rundown urban district where hoboes tend to congregate, coined by Sinclair Lewis. WE

hobosexual *n.* (hobo + homosexual) A person with transient sexual habits, exchanging one sex partner for another frequently and indiscriminately. JA

hoggerel *n.* (hog + doggerel) Vulgar songs or poetry. MBD

hoke *n.* (haze + smoke) A blend of haze and smoke. FW

hokum *n.* (hocus-pocus + bunkum) Something worthless, nonsensical, or untrue. WWA

Hollywoodenhead *n.* (Hollywood + wooden head) A derisive name for a resident of Hollywood, or for someone connected with the movie industry. NA

Holocator *brand name* Golfer's training aid, United Ventures, Inc. TND

Homade *brand name* Sauces, Sona & Hollen Foods, Inc. BTC

hometel *n.* (home + hotel) A hotel featuring apartment-like suites; a tourist home. BDC

homocidious *adj.* (homicide + insidious) Murderously cunning. Coined by H. L. Mencken. AL

homonymble *n.* (homonym + nimble) A pun based upon a homonym, a word sounding the same as another, but with a different meaning. One example concerns the bookkeeper who wore out the seat of his pants, *notwithstanding.* IPE

Honglomerate *n.* (Hong Kong + conglomerate) A multi-national corporation with its headquarters in the Far East. JA

hoolivan *n.* (hooligan + van) A police van equipped with cameras and video equipment, used to monitor crowd behavior at sporting events, etc. OED

horrorscope *n.* (horror + horoscope) A frightening horoscope; a forecast of dire events. DS

Hortisculptures *brand name* Sculptures containing living plants, Brastoff Designs, Inc. BTC

Hotray *brand name* Electric food warmers, Salton, Inc. BTC

hozey *n.* (honey + floozy) A woman of loose morals who is somewhat slovenly in appearance, but affectionate in nature. DAS

huggle *vb.* (hug + snuggle) To cuddle or nestle comfortably with another. FW

Hugliest *brand name* Pantyhose, Special T Hosiery Co. BTC

humalin *n.* (human + insulin) Insulin that is effective in treating diseases of the human body, and which has been manufactured by means of genetic engineering. BAR

Humanals *brand name* Soft-sculpture dolls, Randy & Co., Inc. TND

humanation *n.* (human + automation) The process of tailoring human resources to the requirements of automation. SEL

humaniac *n.* (humane + maniac) An overly zealous animal rights activist.

humgumption *n.* (humbug + gumption) An exaggerated sense of self-importance; nonsense. DS

huminal *n.* (human + animal) A researcher who seeks to develop methods of communication between humans and animals. JA

humint *n.* (human + intelligence) Military slang for intelligence information gathered by humans, as opposed to information gathered electronically. SL

humiture *n.* (humidity + temperature) A composite index that measures the effect of humidity and temperature on the human body.

Also known as the heat-stress index, its cold weather equivalent is the wind-chill factor. SEL

humongous *adj.* (huge + monstrous) Exceptionally large. DD

huppie *n.* (hippie + yuppie) A yuppie who chooses to live an upwardly mobile and also somewhat unconventional lifestyle. SL

huskiing *n.* (husky + skiing) A winter sport in which a team of huskies pulls a person equipped with snow skis. WO

hygristor *n.* (hygrometer + resistor) An electrical resistor in which the resistance varies with humidity. Hygristors are usually a major component in hygrometers, which are instruments for measuring humidity. DST

ibsenity *n.* (Ibsen + obscenity) A play dealing with distasteful or disagreeable subjects. Many of the 19th century Norwegian dramatist Henrik Ibsen's plays included realistic and often scandalous portrayals of sensitive social problems. DS

Identikit *n.* (identification + kit) Trademark name for a means of identifying criminals by creating composite photographs which are an assemblage of individual features selected by witnesses from a variety of drawings. BPF

identikit *n.* (identical + kit) An item produced by means of routine assembly of stock materials, the result being notably stereotyped in form. WES

idylatry *n.* (idyl + idolatry) The worship of nature. OE

ignostic *n.* (ignorant + agnostic) A person who believes there is a way of knowing the truth without empiric proof. SEL

imagineering *n.* (imagine + engineering) Engineering and design through the use of computer graphics, in which it is presumed that one's imagination represents the only limit to what can be achieved. A person who undertakes such work is often refered to as an **imagineer**. BNE

immateur *n.* (immature + amateur) A professional athlete whose career is characterized by outbursts of petulant, immature behavior, either during competitive events or in their personal life.

Immencils *brand name* Mascara, Lancome. BTC

immittance *n.* (impedance + admittance) A characteristic of instruments of transmission or measurement, the function of which is to either impede or admit that which is being transmitted or measured. WE

Immunitea *brand name* Herbal tea, Unitea Herbs. BTC

Impereal *brand name* Vanilla, Lotus Mfg. Co. BTC

imperviable *adj.* (impermeable + impervious) Not permeable; not allowing entrance or passage through. WE

impittious *adj.* (impetuous + pitiless) In reckless haste. Used by Shakespeare in *Hamlet* to describe Laertes' reaction to the death of Ophelia. IPE

impixlocated *adj.* (intoxicated + pixilated) Drunk. DS

incestry *n.* (incest + ancestry) Ancestral heritage that includes incestuous conduct.

Indocrat *n.* (independent + Democrat) A member of the Democratic Party who is inclined to take an independent or non-partisan stance on many issues. BL

Industriever *brand name* Storage and retrieval systems, Kardex Systems, Inc. BTC

inebriety *n.* (inebriation + ebriety) Intoxication. WE

Infantent *brand name* Oxygen equipment, Mistogen Equipment Co. BTC

infanticipate *vb.* (infant + anticipate) To look forward to the birth of a child. Coined by Walter Winchell. AL

Infantoy *brand name* Toys, Alabe Products, Inc. BTC

Infantray *brand name* Nursery organizer, A-Plus Products, Inc. BTC

infernoise *n.* (infernal + noise) An infernal amount of noise. TM

Inflatoy *brand name* Pre-inflated toys, Alvimar Mfg. Co., Inc. BTC

infomaniac *n.* (information + maniac) A person obsessed with trivial facts and information.

infopreneur *n.* (information + entrepreneur) A person engaged in the field of information technology. NW

informance *n.* (informal or inform + performance) Performance art in which a spokesperson, narrator, or artist speaks to the audience about aspects of the work being presented. AM

informercial *n.* (information + commercial) A semi-documentary feature of varying length, typically shown on cable television, combining general information on a particular topic with a subtle promotional message from a commercial sponsor. Also spelled *infomercial.* NWD

infotainment *n.* (information + entertainment) Television programming which is intended to be educational or informative in content, but also dramatic in the style of its presentation. DJ

innoventure *n.* (innovative + venture) A venture, especially one involving finance or investment, which is innovative or unconventional. NW

inscrewtable *adj.* (screw + inscrutable) Film industry jargon for a pornographic movie which features Oriental women. JA

Insectape *brand name* Insecticides, Hercon Laboratories Corp. BTC

Insectocutor *brand name* Insect electrocutor, Hercon Laboratories Corp. TND

insinuendo *n.* (insinuation + innuendo) A veiled allusion or rumor which subtly discredits a person's character or reputation. WE

Inspirease *brand name* Inhaler, Key Pharmaceuticals, Inc. BTC

Instalbum *brand name* Photo albums, Hudson Photographic Industries, Inc. BTC

Instamatic *brand name* Cameras, projectors and film, Eastman Kodak Co. BTC

Instantan *brand name* Tanning aid, Professional Aids Corp. BTC

Instantea *brand name* Instant tea, Redco Foods, Inc. BTC

Insulectric *brand name* Paint, Standard T Chemical Co., Inc. BTC

integraph *n.* (integration + graph) A device used to complete a mathematical integration by graphical methods. DST

intelligentleman *n.* (intelligent + gentleman) A man who is equally respected for his impeccable manners and his intellectual ability. Coined by Walter Winchell. AL

Intellivision *brand name* Video game, Mattel, Inc. TND

interrobang *n.* (interrogation point + bang) A punctuation mark intended for use after exclamatory rhetorical questions such as "Why me?" The interrobang is represented as an exclamation point superimposed over a question mark, and borrows the source word *bang* from printer's slang for an exclamation point. WE

Intimints *brand name* Chocolate, Intimint Chocolate. BTC

intrinsicate *adj.* (intrinsic + intricate) That which is complex and also hidden or internal in nature. It appears in the last act of William Shakespeare's *Antony & Cleopatra*, during the scene in which Cleopatra holds the asp to her breast: "With thy sharp teeth this knot intrinsicate / Of life at once untie."

Invisibleach *brand name* Facial hair bleach, Gambine Products, Inc. BTC

irage *n.* (Iran + rage) The national feeling of rage and hostility toward Iran which was expressed by Americans during the 1979 embassy hostage crisis. WO

irregardless *adj.* (irrespective + regardless) Without regard; heedless. WSC

Irrezestables *brand name* Frozen entrees, Stouffer Foods Corp. BTC

isolite *n.* (isolate + lite) A particular replay technique during televised sports events which was briefly popular in the mid–1970s, in which an individual player appeared in a ring of light, while other players were shown in a visible, but dimmer, background. SBD

itchitate *vb.* (itch + irritate) To irritate by causing an itch; the act of irritating in a particularly annoying manner. MBN

jackelope *n.* (jack rabbit + antelope) A legendary horned rabbit of the American West, reputed to be a hybrid of the jackrabbit and the antelope. Proof of the existence of the jackelope consists mainly of spurious photographs produced for the benefit of tourists, plus occasional exhibits of jackrabbits mounted as trophies, complete with sets of antelope horns jutting from their heads.

Jacobethan *n.* (Jacobean + Elizabethan) A style of architecture utilized in the design of many of the private homes built in the United States between 1890 and 1920. Blending traditional English Elizabethan and Jacobean characteristics, including the use of rough stucco exteriors and half-timber framing, this style has also been called the "Tudor" or "Medieval Revival" style of architecture. AS

Jagwire *brand name* Wheels, Permacast Corp. BTC

Jambrosia *brand name* Fruit spread, Emma's. TNT

jamocha *n.* (java + mocha) A slang term for coffee. WE

Japanazi *n.* (Japanese + Nazi) Military slang used in World War II to designate a military operation by combined Japanese and Nazi forces. DAS

jargantuan *adj.* (jargon + gargantuan) A word describing the task of keeping pace with the constantly changing jargon of modern language; the nature of the task of translating works written in professional jargon into plain English. AT

jargonaut *n.* (jargon + argonaut) A person who uses, creates, or attempts to define jargon. SE

jargoneer *n.* (jargon + engineer) A person adept at creating or using jargon; a jargonaut. OL

jarming *vb.* (jogging + arm) Strenuous and prolonged exercise of the upper body, a regimen considered by many to be as beneficial to cardiovascular fitness as jogging. NW

jasponyx *n.* (jasper + onyx) Onyx containing layers which are partly or entirely jasper. WE

jawbation *n.* (jaw + jobation) A long, tiresome reproof, a *jobation* being a harangue or lecture. WE

jazzetry *n.* (jazz + poetry) Poetry which is read aloud to the accompaniment of jazz music. OED

jeepney *n.* (jeep + jitney) A jeep converted into a jitney bus, a type of vehicle popular in the Philippines. SEL

jetevator *n.* (jet + elevator) A ring-shaped deflector around the exhaust of a rocket engine which can be swiveled to re-direct the rocket exhaust, thus altering the direction of thrust. OED

Jewfro *n.* (Jew + Afro) A long, curly, full-bodied style of wearing one's hair, similar to an Afro. ND

jingle-bellegant *adj.* (jingle bells + elegant) Elegantly dressed in a style or color appropriate to the Christmas season. SEL

jivernacular *adj.* (jive + vernacular) Characteristic of the informal language used among blacks. AM

jocoserious *adj.* (jocose + serious) That which is both funny and serious at the same time. MBD

jollop *n.* (jolly + dollop) A drink of liquor. NTC

jolly bean *n.* (jolly + jelly bean) Drug slang for any stimulant taken orally as a pill or capsule. JA

judder *vb.* (jar + shudder) To vibrate intensely, a word often used to describe the vibration of aircraft engines. WE

Judicare *n.* (judicial + care) A government-sponsored program in which free legal services are provided to the poor. BAR

jummix *vb.* (jumble + mix) To mix together in a confused, disorderly heap. PBW

junt *n.* (joint + chunk) A large amount, or chunk. WE

jurisprude *n.* (jurisprudence + prude) One whose legal opinions are based on severely moralistic or puritanical principles. WE

juvenescence *adj.* (juvenile + adolescence) The state of being or becoming young. Also *juvescence*. OED

kaferita *n.* (kafir + feterita) A hybrid of kafir and feterita, two common varieties of sorghum. WE

Kaleidiskettes *brand name* Colored floppy diskettes, Allenbach Industries, Inc. BTC

kangarooster *n.* (kangaroo + rooster) Australian slang for an amusing or eccentric person. DS

Kanorado *n.* (Kansas + Colorado) A city on the border of Kansas and Colorado. AL

Kensee *n.* (Kentucky + Tennessee) A city on the border of Kentucky and Tennessee. NA

Kentuckiana *n.* (Kentucky + Indiana) A colloquial name for the metropolitan area along the border of Kentucky and Indiana, including the city of Louisville, Kentucky. Despite the widespread acceptance of Kentuckiana as a label that promotes regional identity, some residents still prefer alternatives such as the self-deprecating "Indy-Yucky."

kerseymere *n.* (kersey + cassimere) A fine woolen fabric with a close nap, similar to kersey or cassimere wool. WE

kidult *n.* (kid + adult) A television industry term for that portion of the viewing audience between the ages of 12 and 34. NWD

kip *n.* (kilo + pound) A unit of weight equal to one thousand pounds. WE

kissletoe *n.* (kiss + mistletoe) The mistletoe, a reference to the popular custom of offering kisses beneath a hanging sprig of mistletoe at Christmas. BL

klavern *n.* (Klan + cavern) A unit of the Ku Klux Klan; a place where such a group might meet. WE

kleagle *n.* (Klan + eagle) A high-ranking officer in the hierarchy of the Ku Klux Klan. WE

Klonclave *n.* (Klan + conclave) A regular meeting of members of the Ku Klux Klan. BAI

Klonvocation *n.* (Klan + convocation) The supreme governing body of the Ku Klux Klan. BAI

Kloran *n.* (Klan + Koran) A sacred book which spells out the duties, passwords and oaths of the Ku Klux Klan. IH

Knitility *brand name* Knitting bags, Associated Needlecraft Corp. TND

knurl *n.* (knur + gnarl) A small protuberance, excrescence or knob; in Scotland, any short, thickset person. A **knur** is a rough knot or burr in wood. WE

Koalaby *brand name* Stuffed toy, Gund, Inc. TND

lactalbumin *n.* (lactose + albumin) A simple protein contained in milk which is similar to serum albumin, and of high nutritional quality. DST

lamburger *n.* (lamb + hamburger) A hamburger patty made from ground lamb.

lasket *n.* (latchet + gasket) A type of latching used to fasten the sails of a sailboat. WE

laspring *n.* (last + spring) A British dialect word for young salmon. WE

lassitudinarian *n.* (lassitude + latitudinarian) A person in ill health and lethargic spirits. DS

latensification *n.* (latent + intensification) Intensification of a latent photographic image by means of chemical treatment or exposure to light. WE

Lathurn *brand name* Soap dispenser, American Dispenser Co., Inc. BTC

leerics *n.* (leer + lyrics) Sexually suggestive song lyrics. JA

legitimactor *n.* (legitimate + actor) An actor of proven merit. TM

Legtronics *brand name* Pantyhose, Brevoni Hosiery. BTC

Leisuramics *brand name* Art molds, Gare, Inc. BTC

Leisurest *brand name* Upholstered couches, Imperial Leather Furniture Co. BTC

lemoncholy *adj.* (lemon + melancholy) In a state of melancholia. Created by a transposition of letters, lemoncholy is also a pun in the sense that it aptly describes someone with a "sour disposition." DS

leopon *n.* (leopard + lion) The offspring of a leopard and a lioness. BAR

leotites *n.* (leotard + tights) A garment providing close-fitting coverings for both the body and legs, usually worn during dance or exercise. OWW

Levelawn *brand name* Rake and leveler, Cushman. BTC

lewdity *n.* (lewd + nudity) Nudity, especially when presented in a frankly sexual way.

libratory *n.* (library + laboratory) A university facility combining the functions of a research laboratory with that of a research library. WWA

lidar *n.* (light + radar) A device or system for locating objects. Similar to radar, lidar operates by emitting pulsed laser light instead of microwaves. WES

liger *n.* (lion + tiger) The hybrid of a female tiger and a male lion. Normally the result of interbreeding among circus animals, these hybrid cats may also be called **tiglons** or **tigons**, depending on the sex of the parents. Back-crossing a liger with a tiger results in still another hybrid, known as a **tili**. WE

Lightarget *brand name* Archery target, Bear Archery. BTC

limequat *n.* (lime + kumquat) A hybrid of the lime and kumquat. WE

Limitimer *brand name* Timer for public speakers, D'San Corp. BTC

limon *n.* (lime + lemon) A hybrid of the lime and lemon. WE

Liquidose *brand name* Food products, California-Omega Foods. BTC

Liquifry *brand name* Fish food, Aquarium Products, Inc. BTC

Lockits *brand name* Combination locks, U.S. Fiberglass, Inc. BTC

Loctagons *brand name* Educational toys, Lauri, Inc. BTC

Logoptics *n.* (logo + optics) The trademark of a pictorial sign system that has been proposed as a means of replacing verbal language with a simple, universal system. DJ

lordolatry *n.* (idolatry + lord) Title worship; admiration for a person based solely on that person's social rank. TGP

Louisvillain *n.* (Louisville + villain) A native of Louisville, Kentucky. Coined by H. L. Mencken. AL

lovertine *n.* (love + libertine) A person devoted to the art of love-making, a word attributed to English dramatist Thomas Dekker. MBD BL

loxygen *n.* (liquid + oxygen) Liquid oxygen. WE

Lubath *brand name* Bath oil, Warner-Lambert Co. BTC

lumbersome *adj.* (lumber + cumbersome) Ponderous or clumsy; cumbersome. WE

lumpshious *adj.* (lovely + scrumptious) Extremely delicious, or delightful in appearance. DS

luncheon *n.* (lunch + nuncheon) A light lunch. The root word **nuncheon** dates from the 14th century. AL

lunk *n.* (line + trunk) In telecommunications, an access line that terminates in an automatic dial exchange, where it functions as an access line for subscribers, and as a trunk line for the automatic dial exchange equipment. DST

lupper *n.* (lunch + supper) An afternoon meal, considered either a late lunch or an early supper. YNW

luptious *adj.* (voluptuous + delicious) Having an appearance of loveliness and delight. DS

Luxuray *brand name* Pocket flashlights, Accutec, Inc. BTC

Lyrichord *brand name* Recording label, Lyrichord Discs, Inc. BTC

lyrichord *n.* (lyric + chord) A bowed keyboard instrument featuring rotating wheels connected to a clock mechanism, and having both gut and metal strings. MI

M

McGovernment *n.* (McGovern + government) The political agenda of 1972 presidential candidate George McGovern. JO

machodrama *n.* (macho + melodrama) A movie or play which glorifies aggressive maleness. ND

macon *n.* (mutton + bacon) Mutton which has been salted and cured so as to resemble bacon, a staple food in wartime Britain. YNW

maddle *vb.* (mad + addle) To make crazy or confused. WE

Madhattaner *n.* (mad hatter + Manhattan) A derisive slang label for any person crazy enough to live in Manhattan. NA

magalog *n.* (magazine + catalog) A store-sponsored magazine combining regular magazine features with catalog listings and product information. NW

Magicall *brand name* Automatic telephone dialer, Dasa Corp. BTC

Magicap *brand name* Hair-frosting cap, The Bobby Co. BTC

Magicare *brand name* Stainless steel polish, Apple Polishes, Inc. BTC

Magicleaner *brand name* Rug and upholstery cleaner, Magicleaner Co. BTC

Magicloud *brand name* Foundation garments, Youthcraft-Charmfit. BTC

Magicolor *brand name* Slates, Samuel Lowe Co. BTC

Magicopy *brand name* Carbon copy sets, Gowdy Kolated Products, Inc. BTC

Magicrayon *brand name* Writing products, Magic Marker Industries, Inc. BTC

Magicube *brand name* Flashbulbs, General Electric Co. BTC

Magicut *brand name* Files and saws, Cooper Tools. BTC

magnalium *n.* (magnesium + aluminum) A light aluminum-based alloy also containing some magnesium. OED

magnetron *n.* (magnet + electron) A vacuum tube in which the flow of electrons is regulated by magnetic force to generate microwave force. NWE

magniloquent *adj.* (magnificent + eloquent) Characteristic of a grandiose public address. TGP

magnistor *n.* (magnetic + transistor) A device that utilizes the effects of magnetic fields in semiconductors. DST

magpiety *n.* (magpie + piety) The form of piety that is represented by vocal affirmations, but not substantiated by pious deeds. OED

malaphor *n.* (malaprop + metaphor) A mixed metaphor. IPE

Manglish *n.* (man + English) Written or spoken English which is characterized by sexist language. DD

Manimal *n.* (man + animal) The title of a 1983 television series, concerning a police detective who could change into animal shapes at will.

manit *n.* (man + minute) A measurement of work, being the amount of work which can be done by one man in one minute. MBD

mankey *n.* (man + monkey) A hypothetical hybrid resulting from the mating of a monkey and a human being; the "missing link," the intermediate step between man and monkey on the evolutionary ladder. NWE

manscape *n.* (man + landscape) A picture of a crowd, or a sea of faces in a crowd. OED

Manwich *brand name* Sandwich sauce, Hunt-Wesson Foods, Inc. BTC

mappen *adv.* (may + happen) English dialect term, meaning "may hap" or "perchance." WE

Mardi Grass *n.* (Mardi Gras + grass) A colloquial name for the artificial turf used in the New Orleans Superdome. Because of the regional rivalry between that facility and Houston's Astrodome, Mardi Grass is preferred over the more conventional "Astroturf."

maridelic *adj.* (marijuana + psychedelic) Pertaining to the drug culture of the 1960s. BAI

marijuanaful *adj.* (marijuana + wonderful) Pertaining to indulgence in high-quality marijuana, or any experience that is judged to be unusually good or pleasurable. NTC

marline *n.* (marl + line) A small cord made from two loosely twisted rope strands, which is then wound around the end of a rope or cable to prevent fraying. DST

martempering *n.* (martensite + tempering) A process of quenching hot steel in heated water before cooling to room temperature. In metallurgy, martensite is hot steel that has been quenched in cold water. WE

Marvelustre *brand name* Paint, Cotter & Co. BTC

Masteps *brand name* Mast-climbing device for sailboats, Masteps Corp. TND

matax *n.* (mattock + ax) An ax and a mattock combined in one tool; a pickax. WE

Maternitea *brand name* Herbal tea, Unitea Herbs. BTC

mathemagician *n.* (mathematics + magician) A person who is apparently able to perform magic with numbers or mathematical formulae. TM

Matrays *brand name* Trays, Convergence Corp. BTC

matterate *vb.* (matter + maturate) To make ripe or mature. WE

mattergy *n.* (matter + energy) A word expressing the Einsteinian theory that matter is energy, particularly when referring to subatomic particles. WSC

maximin *adj.* (maximum + minimum) Characteristic of a strategy which maximizes the smallest gain that a participant in a game or competition can guarantee himself. OED

meacock *n.* (meek + peacock) A cowardly or effeminate man. WE

meaconing *n.* (misleading + beaconing) A system for receiving electromagnetic signals and then rebroadcasting them in the same frequency. DST

meatlegger *n.* (meat + bootlegger) A person who illegally markets rationed or restricted meat. NWE

Mechanimals *brand name* Toy animals, The Toy Group. BTC

mechatronics *n.* (mechanical + electronics) That field of engineering which seeks to synthesize computers with mechanical engineering in order to introduce automation to industrial processes. NWD

mediamorphosis *n.* (media + metamorphosis) Distortion or alteration of factual information by the media. BAR

Medicare *n.* (medical + care) A federal health insurance program for persons 65 and over, instituted in the United States as part of the Social Security program in 1965. WE

Medicase *brand name* Medical kit for travelers, Sharon Specialty Products. BTC

Medichair *brand name* Reclining wheelchairs, Trans-Aid Corp. BTC

medichair *n.* (medical + chair) A chair with electronic sensors attached, allowing the medical condition of a person sitting in the chair to be monitored. BAR

megalopolitan *adj.* (megalopolis + metropolitan) Pertaining to very large metropolitan areas. BAI

meld *vb., n.* (melt + weld) To merge; a fabric formed from manmade fibers with an outer sheath which has been melted to bind the fibers together. OED

melodica *n.* (melodic + harmonica) A small wind instrument that is similar to a harmonica, but with a piano-like keyboard. BAR

memistor *n.* (memory + resistor) A non-magnetic memory device used in computers to raise or lower the electrical resistance in response to fluctuations in electrical current. DST

Memorase *brand name* Eraser, U.V. P., Inc. BTC

meniable *adj.* (menial + amiable) Meekly compliant. Coined by Lewis Carroll.

Mentalert *brand name* Prescription drug, Keen Pharmaceuticals, Inc. BTC

Mercandescent *brand name* Lamp, Public Service Lamp Corp. BTC

Mesopolonica *n.* (Mesopotamia + Salonica) British military slang for an unknown destination somewhere along the Eastern Front in World War I. What was then Mesopotamia is now Iraq, while Salonica is now the modern Greek city of Thessaloníki — these roughly corresponded to the easternmost and westernmost limits of the front. DS

Metalanguage *brand name* Recording label, Jazz Composers Orchestra Associates, Inc. BTC

metalanguage *n.* (metal + language) A computer language such as COBOL, in which a set of symbols or words is used to describe another language. DOC

Metalast *brand name* Repair and maintenance material for boats, Woolsey Marine Industries. BTC

Metalastic *brand name* Waterproofing, The 3E Group, Inc. BTC

Metaleaf *brand name* Aluminum paint, PPG Industries. BTC

Metalloy *brand name* Auto body filler, M & H Laboratories. BTC

methodolatry *n.* (method + idolatry) An excessive and impractical interest in methods. DNW

Metrinch *brand name* Wrenches and wrench sets, Surelab Superior Research Laboratories, Inc. TND

Metrollopis *n.* (metropolis + trollop) The city of London. Also, as **Metrollop**, a colloquial name for the Metropole Hotel. DS

metropollyana *n.* (metropolitan + Pollyana) The erroneous belief that everyone will eventually move to cities and suburbs, a doctrine often used to support policies that discriminate against rural areas. WO

metropolypus *n.* (metropolis + polypus) A metropolitan area which grows without restraint in all directions. **Polypus** is the name of a genus of octopus. BL

Mexicali *n.* (Mexico + California) A city in Mexico, located on the border with California. AL

Mexicancellation *n.* (Mexican + cancellation) A Mexican divorce. DA

Mexicatessan *brand name* Mexican food products, Ruiz Food Products, Inc. BTC

mexicola *n.* (Mexico + cola) A cocktail containing cola and tequila. BG

Mexicorn *brand name* Corn, Green Giant Co. BTC

Michigander *n.* (Michigan + gander) The colloquial name given to a native or resident of the state of Michigan, a word attributed to Abraham Lincoln. WE BL

Michillinda *n.* (Michigan + Illinois + Indiana) A city in northern California, founded by settlers who had moved there from the states of Michigan, Illinois and Indiana. NOL

middlescence *n.* (middle + obsolescence) A form of age discrimination in which persons are made to feel archaic or incompetent once they reach middle age. BNE

Mildoom *brand name* Mildew-proofing paint additives, Proctor Paint & Varnish Co. BTC

milicrat *n.* (military + bureaucrat) A military bureaucrat. SL

milkstache *n.* (milk + mustache) The residue left on the upper lip after drinking deeply from a glass of milk. FW

milliammeter *n.* (milliampere + meter) An instrument for measuring electric current in milliamperes. WE

millionheiress *n.* (millionaire + heiress) A female heir to great wealth. DA

mimsy *adj.* (miserable + flimsy) Unhappy; in an emotional state characterized by misery and sensitivity to one's own plight. Coined by Lewis Carroll. AA

mingy *adj.* (mean + stingy) Mean-tempered and avaricious. WE

Minniapple *n.* (mini + apple) A nickname for the city of Minneapolis, Minnesota, coined as a wry, self-deprecating comparison to New York City, which proudly calls itself "The Big Apple."

Miracloth *brand name* All-purpose cleaning cloth, Chicapee. BTC

mirthquake *n.* (mirth + earthquake) Entertainment resulting in convulsive mirth. OED

mizzle *n.* (mist + drizzle) Precipitation characterized by a combination of mist and light rain. WE

mizzle *vb.* (moan + grizzle) To complain or whimper. OED

mobot *n.* (motor + robot) A mobile, motorized robot. WSC

moccasock *n.* (moccasin + sock) A type of indoor footwear, consisting of a woolen sock with a soft leather sole. DNW

mockabre *adj.* (mock + macabre) Grimly horrible in a ridiculously unsuitable manner. BAI

mocktail *n.* (mock + cocktail) A name for any non-alcoholic mixed drink.

modacrylic *n.* (modified + acrylic) A kind of synthetic fiber used in clothing and wigs. OED

mog *vb.* (move + jog) To move slowly from one place to another. WE

Moistop *brand name* Flashing, Fortifier Corp. TND

Moistureyes *brand name* Skin moisturizer for around the eyes, Westport Laboratories. BTC

molectronics *n.* (molecular + electronics) That branch of electronics which concerns the production of complex electronic circuits reduced to micro-miniature size. DST

momentaneous *adj.* (moment + spontaneous) Of a transitory character. Also: **momentaneity.** OED

monergy *n.* (money + energy) A theory that equates money with energy, particularly when in the form of savings or investments. The concept of monergy is typically promoted during campaigns encouraging bank depositors to save more of their earnings, comparing the benefits of monetary savings to those of energy conservation. NW

Monstickers *brand name* Stickers, Henry Gordy International, Inc. BTC

monstracious *adj.* (monstrous + ferocious) Distinctive because of size and ferocity. OTW

moondoggle *n.* (moon + boondoggle) A derisive name for the enormous financial resources which would be required to explore the moon. Some aerospace engineers believe such an expenditure would be a colossal waste of resources, which should instead be allocated to other space projects they feel are more worthwhile or cost-efficient. DJ

Moorth *n.* (moon + earth) The primeval body that split apart to form the earth and moon. Also: **Earthoon.** BAI

Moosevelt *n.* (moose + Roosevelt) The nickname given to Theodore Roosevelt when he campaigned as a candidate of the Progressive Party during the 1912 election. The party's emblem at that time was the bull moose. BL

mosaiculture *n.* (mosaic + culture) In gardening, an arrangement of small plants of different colors in a pattern resembling a carpet. OED

Mosquitone *brand name* Insect repellent, MK Laboratories. BTC

motel *n.* (motor + hotel) A hotel intended for use primarily by persons traveling by car. First used in California in 1925, the word **motel** eventually prevailed over alternatives such as **autel** and **autotel.** WE YNW

motelodge *n.* (motel + lodge) A variation on the word **motel**, usually intended to convey the impression that the accommodations are more comfortable than those to be found at an ordinary "motel." BNE

motopia *n.* (motor + utopia) An urban environment which has been designed to accommodate the needs of pedestrians by carefully restricting motorized traffic. OED

motorail *n.* (motor + rail) A service in which automobiles, their drivers and passengers are transported by rail. OED

motorama *n.* (motor + panorama) A popular promotional name for an exhibition of motor vehicles. OED

Motoraser *brand name* An erasing machine, Keuffel & Esser Co. BTC

motorcade *n.* (motorcar + cavalcade) A procession of automobiles. DAS

Motown *n.* (motor + town) The city of Detroit, Michigan, also called "Motor City" because of the large automobile industries based there. **Motown** became famous as the name of a Detroit-based record company responsible for a series of hit recordings during the 1960s and '70s. BNE

mounce *n.* (metric + ounce) A unit of mass equal to 25 grams, or about one ounce. DST

mousewife *n.* (mouse + housewife) A woman who is completely subordinate to the will of her husband. BAI

movelist *n.* (movie + novelist) A person who writes for the movies. SEL

movideo *n.* (movie + video) A feature-length film comprised mainly of concert performances. NWD

mudge *vb.* (move + budge) To budge; to move. WE

mugid *adj.* (muggy + humid) Weather which is hot, damp and close. FW

Multimate *brand name* Computer software, Multimate International Corp. BTC

multiversity *n.* (multiple + university) A large university with many component schools, colleges, academic divisions, and functions. WES

Mummerset *n.* (mummer + Somerset) British slang for the fake rural accent which is typically adopted by actors appearing as English provincial characters. Mummerset is the imaginary rustic county in the west of England which actors identify as the source of this particular accent. A **mummer** is a theatrical performer. DJ

Muppet *n.* (marionette + puppet) The group of puppet-like characters created by puppeteer Jim Henson, and popular for their appearances on the children's television series *Sesame Street*. Henson always claimed that he chose the name at random, but explained it as a blend of marionette and puppet to satisfy interviewers who insisted on knowing where the word came from.

Musicakes *brand name* Device for making cakes play music when cut, Seagren Enterprises. TND

Musicards *brand name* Music game/learning aid, Cramer Products Co. BTC

musicassette *n.* (music + cassette) A tape cassette of pre-recorded music. OED

Musicenter *brand name* Stereo systems, Sanyo Fisher USA Corp. BTC

Musicleaner *brand name* Record cleaner, Recoton Corp. BTC

musicomedy *n.* (music + comedy) A musical comedy. TM

mux *n.* (mix + flux) A blend of varied thoughts flowing through one's head. BAI

mythistory *n.* (myth + history) An historical account which mingles fables and legends with facts. OED

N

namesmanship *n.* (names + gamesmanship) Distinctive skill in the art of name-dropping. OED

napalm *n.* (naphthene + palmitate) A jellied gasoline compound used in incendiary bombs and other weapons. WSC

narcoma *n.* (narcotic + coma) A deep sleep induced by narcotics. BAI

natter *vb.* (nag + chatter) To find fault or complain incessantly. DCS

Naturalamb *brand name* Prophylactics, Carter-Wallace, Inc. BTC

Naturalamp *brand name* Lamps, Interdesign, Inc. BTC

Naturalash *brand name* Fake eyelashes, Beautee Sense, Inc. BTC

Naturalean *brand name* Food substitutes, Sopro Foods, Inc. BTC

Naturescape *brand name* Wildflower seeds, Applewood Seed Co. BTC

Naturest *brand name* Pharmaceutical, Nature Way Products, Inc. BTC

Naussie *n.* (new + Aussie) Australian slang for a newly arrived emigrant. DS

Nauticolors *brand name* Boat repair and maintenance material, Woolsey Marine Industries. BTC

Neatip *brand name* Shoelaces, St. Louis Braid Co. BTC

neatnik *n.* (neat + beatnik) An individual whose personal habits and appearance are exceedingly meticulous. OED

Nectarose *brand name* Rose wine, The Seagram Wine Co. BTC

needcessity *n.* (need + necessity) Necessity. Attributed to Sir Walter Scott. WE

negatron *n.* (negative + electron) An electron. WE

negentropy *n.* (negative + entropy) A blending of **negative entropy,** a numerical measure of information content. OED

nerd *n.* (nerts + turd) An unpleasant, unattractive, unstylish, or insignificant person. **Nerts** was a popular colloquial variation of the interjection "nuts" during the 1950s and '60s. WES

Neurope *n.* (new + Europe) A word coined in 1919 to describe the new political, economic and geographic alignment of the countries of Europe following the first World War. DS

Neverinkle *brand name* Rubber cement, Dick Blick Co. BTC

Neverip *brand name* Eraser, Weber Costello. BTC

newelty *n.* (new + novelty) A novelty. BL

Newfanglia *n.* (newfangled + Anglia) A hypothetical locale in modern England, characterized by widespread technological change and rampant consumerism. DA

Newmania *n.* (Newman + mania) Enthusiastic support for the beliefs of Cardinal John Henry Newman, a prominent 19th century English theologian and leader of the Oxford Movement. OED

newspepper *n.* (newspaper + pepper) Journalistic jargon for a celebrity or official who can be counted on to provide an appropriate quote when needed to pep up a dull edition of a newspaper. JA

newszine *n.* (news + magazine) A fan magazine that is typically composed entirely of facts and information and excludes amateur fiction. DJ

newt *n.* (new + recruit) A new workman or soldier; a novice. DAS

newtique *n.* (new + boutique) Advertising coinage, meant to give the impression that a particular store handles only the latest fashions. DA

Newyorican *n.* (New York + Puerto Rican) A resident of New York who is of Puerto Rican descent. BNE

Newzak *n.* (news + Muzak) News coverage, the original impact of which has been dulled by repetition. Also spelled **Newszak.** NW

Nichrome *n.* (nickel + chrome) The trademark given to an alloy of nickel, chrome, and sometimes, iron. BNW

nickelodeon *n.* (nickel + melodeon) A turn-of-the-century theater which showed motion pictures for the price of a nickel. The film was usually accompanied by live music from a **melodeon** or **melodion,** a keyboard instrument also known as the "American organ." WE

nicotunia *n.* (nicotine + petunia) A hybrid of the petunia and the tobacco plant, developed and named by American botanist Luther Burbank. BL

nife *n.* (nickel [Ni] + iron [Fe]) A blended word made up of the chemical symbols for nickel and iron, used to designate ore that contains these two metals. OED

niniversity *n.* (ninny + university) A humorous or derisive name bestowed upon what is presumed to be a university of ninnies. OED

nitch *n.* (nick + notch) A slight notch, break or incision. OED

nitrogation *n.* (nitrogen + irrigation) Irrigation in which measured amounts of anhydrous ammonia fertilizer are added to the irrigating water. A more general term for a method of irrigation in which one or more nutrients are added to the water is **fertigation.** DNW

nobodaddy *n.* (nobody + daddy) A disrespectful name for God, also used to refer to anyone who is no longer held in esteem. Attributed to the English poet William Blake. OED

nonsensational *adj.* (nonsense + sensational) Sensationally nonsensical — a coinage which appears primarily in theatrical reviews. DS

noration *n.* (narration + oration) An announcement, report or rumor. BL

Norlina *n.* (North + Carolina) A city in North Carolina near the Virginia border, its name being a telescoped blend of **North Carolina.** AL

Nosodak *n.* (North Dakota + South Dakota) A blend word used when referring to the two states as one region. AL

Nosquito *brand name* Mosquito repellent, Farnam Co., Inc. BTC

nucleonics *n.* (nucleon + electronics) The branch of science and technology which is concerned with nucleons and the atomic nucleus. OED

nudancer *n.* (nude + dancer) One who dances in the nude. TM

nudgement *n.* (nudge + judgment) In print journalism, the ability to judge whether or not a particular news item is worthy of publication. JA

nukemare *n.* (nuke + nightmare) A sense of foreboding in regard to the onset of thermonuclear war; anxiety regarding the likely occurrence of an environmentally disastrous accident at a nuclear power plant. NW

numberal *n.* (number + numeral) A number. PBW

numberous *adj.* (number + numerous) Numerous. BL

numeracy *n.* (numerate + literacy) The ability to effectively understand and use numbers. OED

nursle *vb.* (nurse + nuzzle) To bring up; nurture. WE

nutarian *n.* (nut + vegetarian) A vegetarian whose diet consists largely of nuts and nut products. OED

nutter *n.* (nut + butter) A substitute for butter, made using oil derived from nuts. OED

obscureaucrat *n.* (obscure + bureaucrat) A government worker whose functions and responsibilities are ambiguous or hidden. Also **obscureaucracy**.

obstipation *n.* (obstinate + constipation) Constipation that is difficult to relieve. DST

occultivated *adj.* (occult + cultivated) Displaying a refined and erudite knowledge of the occult. TM

ocicat *n.* (ocelot + cat) A domestic cat with the distinctive yellow coat and black markings of an ocelot.

Octopush *n.* (octopus + push) An underwater game played in a swimming pool between teams composed of six members. Participants are equipped with snorkel gear, and play involves attempts to push a leaden puck into a submerged goal with wooden or plastic rackets. NW

odditorium *n.* (odd + auditorium) An establishment which specializes in displaying oddities and unusual collectibles. OED

Ohiowa *n.* (Ohio + Iowa) A community in Nebraska which was established by pioneers from Ohio and Iowa. AL

Oilily *brand name* Optical products, Renaissance Eyeware. BTC

olfactronics *n.* (olfactory + electronics) The science of odors and their detection by means of instruments. BNW

Omahogs *n.* (Omaha + hogs) A derisive name given to the residents of Omaha, Nebraska, possibly referring to the stockyards and meat-packing industry of that city. DD

opacifier *n.* (opaque + pacifier) A substance used to treat solid rocket propellant which absorbs heat and light and thus protects the propellant from deterioration. DST

opinionnaire *n.* (opinion + questionnaire) A questionnaire which is intended to determine the opinions of those surveyed. DJ

Optacon *n.* (optical + tactile + converter) A device which allows the blind to recognize printed characters by touching an array of tiny rods, which then vibrate in response to the pattern of light of individual characters. OED

Opticap *brand name* Camera lens cap, Spiratone, Inc. BTC

Opticare *brand name* Optical products, Titmus Optical, Inc. BTC

Opticase *brand name* Optical products, Opticase. BTC

oracy *n.* (oral + literacy) Oral literacy, the ability to hear and speak. BNW

orangelo *n.* (orange + pomelo) A hybrid citrus fruit which is a cross between an orange and a pomelo. WE

oranghetti *n.* (orange + spaghetti) A variety of spaghetti squash, characterized by an orange rind which is similar in color to that of a pumpkin.

orature *n.* (oral + literature) The oral poetry and narrative tradition of a pre-literate people or nation. BAR

Orbitile *brand name* Studded tile, American Floor Products Co. BTC

orchideous *adj.* (orchid + hideous) Characteristic of a decorative scheme which emphasizes the extravagant display of flowers. TM

Organicolor *brand name* Hair care products, Dow Brands. BTC

organiculture *n.* (organic + culture) Gardening or agriculture in which the fertilizer used is entirely organic in origin. DNW

Organicure *brand name* Hair conditioners, Dow Brands. BTC

Organicurl *brand name* Beauty aids, Dow Brands. BTC

Organimals *brand name* Personal care products, Aubrey Organics. BTC

organola *n.* (organ + pianola) An automatic organ invented in 1901, intended for use in small churches, and designed to be played with perforated paper rolls like a pianola. MI

orpharion *n.* (Orpheus + Arion) A stringed musical instrument popular during the Renaissance, similar to a cittern or lute. The word combines the name of Orpheus, a famous musician in Greek mythology, with that of Arion, a Greek poet and musician who lived during the 7th century B.C. WE

ortanique *n.* (orange + tangerine + unique) A hybrid citrus fruit cultivated mainly in the West Indies, and produced by crossing the orange and tangerine. The resulting fruit resembles a slightly flattened orange. OED

ovalbumin *n.* (ova + albumin) The primary form of protein contained in eggwhite. DST

owdacious *adj.* (audacious + outrageous) Impertinent or mischievous. OED

Oxbridge *n.* (Oxford + Cambridge) A collective term for the English universities of Oxford and Cambridge, also referred to as **Camford.** BPF

oysterics *n.* (oyster + hysterics) A morbid fear of eating oysters, based on the belief that they are likely to be infected with the bacterium which causes typhoid fever. DS

Pacessories *brand name* Bicycling apparel, Pace/Cap-It-All. BTC

pajamboree *n.* (pajama + jamboree) Another name for a slumber party. AL

palevent *n.* (paleography + event) A relatively sudden or short-lived event in geologic history. DST

palimony *n.* (pal + alimony) Payments similar to alimony, demanded of certain celebrities by estranged lovers without benefit of wedlock or divorce. DJ

paltripolitan *n.* (paltry + metropolitan) An insular city dweller who has chosen an isolated existence, a life apart from the city's diverse cultural and social life. BYR

pandamonium *n.* (panda + pandemonium) A journalistic reference to the maniacal enthusiasm displayed by the public whenever giant Chinese pandas are exhibited at an American zoo.

Pandorable *brand name* Knit goods, Pandora Sportwear Industries. BTC

Panelense *brand name* Skylights, Naturay Systems Corp. BTC

pang *n.* (pain + sting) A brief, piercing pain. WE

Pantimonium *brand name* Pantyhose, Treo-Fortuna Co. BTC

pantler *n.* (pantry + butler) A servant in charge of the pantry. WE

Pantskin *brand name* Foundation garments, Merit Foundations. BTC

pantsuit *n.* (pants + suit) A woman's suit of clothing, consisting of a long jacket and matching pants. WES

paperalysis *n.* (paper + paralysis) A work stoppage caused by an overwhelming excess of paperwork. YNW

parafango *n.* (paraffin + fango) A mixture of mud and paraffin, used as an external application in the treatment of certain physical ailments such as arthritis and rheumatism. Fango is a particular type of clay mud found in the therapeutic hot springs at Battaglio, Italy. OED

Paralympics *n.* (paraplegic + Olympics) An international sports competition in which the participants are confined to wheelchairs. BNE

parascending *n.* (parachute + ascending) A sport in which parachutists are towed behind a boat or motor vehicle in order to attain a certain height, then released to fall on a predetermined target. OED

parasheet *n.* (parachute + sheet) A simple form of parachute in which the canopy is a single piece of material, or two or more pieces of material sewn together. DST

parashoot *vb.* (parachute + shoot) The act of firing upon parachuting enemy soldiers. The word was coined to describe exercises by the British Home Guard in World War II, who were trained to shoot the paratroops anticipated as the vanguard of a German invasion of England. OED

parathormone *n.* (parathyroid + hormone) A hormone which acts to increase the amount of calcium in the blood. OED

Parisac *brand name* Handbags, Loriet Fashions, Inc. BTC

Paristyle *brand name* Handbags, Paristyle Fashions Enterprises Ltd. BTC

parlambling *n.* (parlance + ambling) Rambling speech. OE

Parrotdise *brand name* Pet products, Pyramid Bird Toys, Inc. BTC

patriotute *n.* (patriot + prostitute) A prostitute who specializes in catering to the needs of servicemen. BAI

peacify *vb.* (peace + pacify) To make calm; pacify. OED

pecurious *adj.* (peculiar + curious) Minutely and scrupulously exact. BL

Pedalift *brand name* Trailer accessory, Reese Products, Inc. BTC

peekture *n.* (peek + picture) A pornographic movie. BAI

pelviscope *n.* (pelvis + scope) An optical instrument used during pelvic examinations. DST

Pencilist *brand name* Telephone indexes, The Bates Mfg. Co. BTC

Penetroil *brand name* Stains and sealers, Enterprise Co. BTC

peninsularity *n.* (peninsula + insularity) A personality characteristic resulting from living on a peninsula, and thus having little contact with people from other lands. OED

pentangle *n.* (pentacle + angle) A pentacle, the five-sided star associated with magical beliefs. OED

pepperidge *n.* (pepper + ridge) The common name given to several varieties of American gum tree. OED

Perfectone *brand name* Marine horns, Signaltone-Neiman, Inc. BTC

periphlebitis *n.* (peripheral + phlebitis) Inflammation of the tissues surrounding a vein. DST

pervaporation *n.* (permeation + evaporation) The evaporation of a liquid through a semi-permeable membrane. OED

perverb *n.* (perverse + proverb) An adage which combines different words or phrases from traditional proverbs in order to convey wry, whimsical or offbeat meanings. Perverbs may juxtapose elements of a familiar saying, as in "In every silver lining, there's a cloud." Or, perverbs may borrow elements from several proverbs, as in "The road to hell is paved with rolling stones." WE

pervertising *n.* (perverted + advertising) Advertising which is characterized by sexual innuendo. BAI

pessimal *adj.* (pessimistic + optimal) That which is likely to produce the worst possible outcome or result. SL

Petcetera *brand name* Pet products, Petcetera, Inc. BTC

Peterloo *n.* (Peter + Waterloo) The name given to a famous confrontation between English troops and protesters which occurred in St. Peter's Fields, Manchester, on August 16, 1819. Cavalry troops were ordered to forcibly disperse a peaceful crowd gathered to demonstrate on behalf of parliamentary reform, causing numerous deaths and injuries.

petishism *n.* (pet + fetishism) An abnormally intense emotional attachment to pets. BNE

petroil *n.* (petrol + oil) A British term referring to the mixture of gasoline and oil required in many two-stroke engines. OED

pettiloon *n.* (pantaloon + petticoat) A woman's undergarment combining the features of an underskirt and tight-fitting pants. DS

Petzels *brand name* Pet products, Famous Fido's Doggie Dell, Inc. BTC

phallacy *n.* (phallus + fallacy) An erroneous belief concerning some aspect of male sexuality. BAI

Phantomachine *brand name* Toy vehicle, Mattel, Inc. BTC

philanthrobber *n.* (philanthropy + robber) One who uses charitable funds in a dishonest or illegal fashion. WWA

philanthropoid *n.* (philanthropist + anthropoid) An adviser on philanthropy, employed by either a government agency or a charitable foundation. OTW

phlizz *n.* (flop + fizzle) A total failure. Coined by English novelist and playwright John Galsworthy. DS

phonestheme *n.* (phoneme + aesthetic) The common element of sound occurring in a group of symbolic words. WE

photomaton *n.* (photo + automaton) A device which automatically takes photographs, usually operated by inserting coins in a slot to activate the camera while the customer is posing inside a curtained booth. OED

photronic *adj.* (photo + electronic) Of or relating to a kind of photovoltaic cell. OED

phreak *n.* (phone + freak) A person who is obsessed with telephones. Also, as in **phreaking**, the mimicking of touch-tone telephone signals in order to make unauthorized toll-free calls. BNE, ND

pianologue *n.* (piano + monologue) A comic monologue accompanied by piano. WE

Picharades *brand name* Game, International Games. BTC

pickering *n.* (pickerel + herring) Another name for a pickerel, a young or small pike. WE

Pickfair *n.* (Pickford + Fairbanks) The name newspapermen gave to the Tudor-style mansion in the hills north of Hollywood once owned by movie stars Mary Pickford and Douglas Fairbanks.

Pictionary *brand name* Game, Western Publishing Co., Inc. BTC

piffle *vb.* (piddle + trifle) To talk or act in a trivial or silly manner. WE

pindling *adj.* (pining + dwindling) A 19th century American dialect word, describing a state of debility in which one is weak, and growing weaker. AET

pinkermint *adj.* (pink + peppermint) Having the pink color of peppermint candy. BAI

pinkler *n.* (pintle + tinkler) A slang name for the penis. **Pintle** has been used as a synonym for **penis** since the 18th century. DS

pinlay *n.* (pin + inlay) In dentistry, inlay work which is held in place by pins. OED

piroot *n.* (pirouette + root) To wander idly; to snoop about from place to place. WE

planacea *n.* (plan + panacea) A strategy which is proposed with assurances that it will solve several problems at once. FW

planetesimal *n.* (planet + infinitesimal) One of the numerous small heavenly bodies which may have existed during the early stages of the solar system. WE

plantimal *n.* (plant + animal) An organism which shares the characteristics of plants and animals. Examples of plantimals include several varieties of slime fungus, and the organisms created when plant and animal cells are fused as a result of genetic engineering. BNE

Plantrainer *brand name* Houseplant trellis, Coneco Plant Care Products. BTC

Plasticlear *brand name* Plastic-finish marine varnish, Boatlife, Inc. BTC

Plasticoat *brand name* Book covers, Colad, Inc. BTC

Plasticolor *brand name* Enamel, Armstrong Paint & Varnish Co., Inc. BTC

Plasticutter *brand name* Acrylic sheet cutter, Craftics, Inc. BTC

Plastinamel *brand name* Plastic enamel, Preservative Paint Co. BTC

platitudinarian *n.* (platitude + latitudinarian) A person who is full of platitudes. MBD

playbore *n.* (playboy + bore) An egomaniacal libertine. Coined by Walter Winchell. WW

Pleasantime *brand name* Adult game, Pacific Game Co. BTC

Pleascent *brand name* Hair permanent, Helene Curtis Industries. BTC

Pleasoning *brand name* Seasonings, Frank & Italiano, Inc. BTC

Pleasurest *brand name* Bedding, Congoleum Corp. BTC

plench *n.* (pliers + wrench) A tool which can perform the functions of a pliers and a wrench, used to make pulling and turning motions in the zero gravity conditions of space flight. WE

plentitude *n.* (plenitude + plenty) A word used erroneously as a synonym for **plenitude**. OED

plodge *vb.* (plod + trudge) To wade or walk heavily. WE

plugola *n.* (plug + payola) Incidental advertising on radio or television which is provided gratis instead of being purchased. WES

plumcot *n.* (plum + apricot) A hybrid of the plum and apricot. WE

plumpendicular *adj.* (plumb + perpendicular) Perpendicular. BL

pluranimity *n.* (plurality + unanimity) A diversity of opinions. OED

Pocketalker *brand name* Personal-communications device for the hearing-impaired, Williams Sound Corp. BTC

pockmanteau *n.* (pocket + portmanteau) A traveling bag equipped with several separate compartments or pockets. OED

poet lariat *n.* (poet laureate + lariat) A title bestowed upon humorist Will Rogers, who became famous for the wry observations concerning contemporary political and social issues he would make while performing rope tricks.

politichine *n.* (political + machine) A political machine; the controlling apparatus of a political party. BL

politricks *n.* (politics + tricks) Underhanded tactics implemented during an election to undermine the campaign of the opposing candidate. TM

Pollenergy *brand name* Bee-pollen food supplement, C. C. Pollen Co. BTC

pollitician *n.* (poll + politician) A politician who rigs the outcome of a poll so that it reflects favorably upon his own campaign. TM

polocrosse *n.* (polo + lacrosse) A game which combines elements of polo and lacrosse, involving players on horseback using sticks similar to those employed in lacrosse to drive a sponge rubber ball into a goal. WE

pomato *n.* (potato + tomato) A hybrid of the potato and the tomato. The resulting plant has the fruit-bearing foliage of the tomato, plus the tuberous roots of the potato. Created and named by American horticulturist Luther Burbank, the pomato is also known as the **potomato** or **topato**. WE

pompass *n.* (pompous + ass) A pompous ass. FW

pompetent *adj.* (pompous + competent) The annoying ability of some persons to be exceedingly pompous and exceedingly competent at the same time. SEL

poncess *n.* (ponce + princess) A woman who supports a man through prostitution. **Ponce** is British slang for a pimp. DS

pondynamics *n.* (ponder + dynamics) Body language which conveys the impression that one is deep in thought, such as furrowing the brow, stroking the chin, etc. JA

popestant *n.* (pope + Protestant) A nonce word for a **papist** or Catholic, a non–Protestant. OED

populuxe *n.* (popular + deluxe) A name given to the era of the late 1950s and early '60s, when the conspicuous consumption of American popular culture combined with a vulgar sense of design to produce an era of rampant kitsch. NWD

pornicator *n.* (porn + fornicator) A purveyor of pornographic materials. JO

pornovelist *n.* (porn + novelist) A writer of pornographic novels. DA

Porschpoiler *brand name* Air-control panels for Porsche automobiles, Target Motorsports. BTC

Portables *brand name* Tables for sailboats, Barnett Zaffron & Associates. BTC

Portabolt *brand name* Portable door lock, Ronde. BTC

portentious *adj.* (portentous + pretentious) Pompous and self-important. OED

portledge *n.* (portage + privilege) The right of way granted to boatmen for transporting boats and supplies overland from one body of water to another. WE

portmantologism *n.* (portmanteau + neologism) A new word which is formed by the union of two words sharing common letters or sounds. BYR

Portrolio *brand name* Artist's carrying case, Multiple Choice. BTC

positron *n.* (positive + electron) A positively charged atomic particle having the same mass and charge as the electron. WE

posolutely *adj.* (positively + absolutely) A slang word used to indicate a high degree of certainty. IPE

possibilitate *vb.* (possible + facilitate) To make possible. TGP

Posterail *brand name* Graphics and photo exhibitor, Struc-Tube. BTC

Posturest *brand name* Back rests, Bell-Horn. BTC

pother *n.* (pain + bother) A noisy disturbance or commotion. WE

potomato *n.* (potato + tomato) A hybrid of the tomato and potato plants. WE

povertician *n.* (poverty + politician) A person who is responsible for administering government poverty programs. BNE

Powerake *brand name* Motorized lawn rake, F.D. Kees Mfg. Co. BTC

Practicalarm *brand name* Fire alarm system, Simplex Time Recorder Co. BTC

preliminate *vb.* (preliminary + eliminate) To undertake an initial process of selection in which those things deemed inferior are discarded. SEL

prequel *n.* (precede + sequel) A film or novel dealing with events which precede those of an existing completed work. OED

presbygational *adj.* (Presbyterian + Congregational) A form of church organization which borrows elements from both the Presbyterian and Congregational churches. BL

Presseal *brand name* Mailing boxes, St. Regis Paper Co. BTC

Pressnap *brand name* Loose-leaf binders, Charles Leonard, Inc. BTC

prevaricaterer *n.* (prevaricate + caterer) A dishonest caterer. BL

Preventamins *brand name* Vitamins, Nature's Way Products, Inc. BTC

Preventime *brand name* Vitamins and minerals, Nutrition Enterprises. BTC

Prevenzyme *brand name* Pharmaceutical, Legere Pharmaceuticals, Inc. BTC

previnder *vb.* (prevent + hinder) Prevent. BL

prickado *vb.* (prick + passado) To thrust or stab with a sword. **Prickado** is used as a humorous variant of **passado,** a forward thrust in fencing. TA

priestianity *n.* (priest + Christianity) Emphasis upon the importance of the office or the power of the priest, often at the expense of religious belief. WE

prillion *n.* (prill + pillion) Tin which has been extracted from slag. **Pillion** is tin which is left in slag after smelting, while **prill** is the act of converting such material into pellet form. WE

pringle *vb.* (prinkle + tingle) To tingle persistently. **Prinkle** is a Scottish dialect word, meaning to prickle or tingle. WE

prinister *n.* (prime + minister) A prime minister. BL

Printongs *brand name* Photography tongs, FR Chemicals. BTC

prissy *adj.* (prim + sissy) Prim and precise; affectedly proper. WE

pritchel *n.* (pritch + prickle) A pointed iron tool commonly used by blacksmiths. A **pritch** is a pointed staff. WE

processorhea *n.* (processor + diarrhea) The tendency of a person using a word processor to adopt an excessively verbose style. NW

prod *n., vb.* (poke + rod) A pointed instrument used to encourage the movement of another, or the act of doing so. WE

profanatic *n.* (profane + fanatic) One who is devoted to the use of profanity. OED

Prohiblican *n.* (Prohibition + Republican) A Republican who supported Prohibition. BL

promptual *adj.* (prompt + punctual) Scrupulously prompt. BL

proprietariat *n.* (proprietary + proletariat) Those persons in a community or social group who are property owners. OED

prostisciutto *n.* (prostitute + prosciutto) A prostitute considered metaphorically as an item on a menu. Coined by the Irish writer Samuel Beckett. OED

Protectone *brand name* Acoustical ceiling tile, The Celotex Corp. BTC

Protectongue *brand name* Harmonicas, Fred Gretsch Enterprises. BTC

prounce *vb.* (prance + flounce) To caper or strut in a flouncing manner. PBW

psychedelicatessan *n.* (psychedelic + delicatessan) An establishment where a variety of hallucinogenic drugs can be obtained. TM

Psychedelicolor *brand name* Artist's paints, Stafford-Reeves, Inc. BTC

Psychedelphia *n.* (psychedelic + Philadelphia) A neighborhood or district where drug use is common, a name once bestowed upon the Haight-Ashbury or "Hashbury" neighborhood of San Francisco. BAI

psychergy *n.* (psychic + energy) Intellectual vitality. BAI

psychiatricky *adj.* (psychiatry + tricky) A movie featuring characters whose actions and motives can be explained fully only by means of a psychiatric evaluation. The psychiatrist's explanation which concludes Alfred Hitchcock's movie *Psycho* is one example of a psychiatricky ending to a movie. WWA

pulmonia *n.* (pulmonary + pneumonia) Pneumonia. BL

Pulmotor *n.* (pulmonary + motor) The trademark name for a device which pumps oxygen, air or a mixture of the two into and out of the lungs. WE

pulsar *n.* (pulsating + star) A cosmic source of radio signals which pulsate intermittently, and which have been attributed to rapidly rotating neutron stars. OED

Pulstar *brand name* Electronic equipment, Pulse Dynamics Mfg. Corp. BTC

Pumpencil *brand name* Pencils, Dur-O-Lite, Inc. BTC

Pumpernibbles *brand name* Snack products, Pepperidge Farm, Inc. BTC

Pupperoni *brand name* Dog treats, The Quaker Oats Co. BTC

Puritea *brand name* Herbal tea, Unitea Herbs. BTC

pursley *n.* (purslane + parsley) Another name for purslane, a common herb. WE

pushency *n.* (push + urgency) Something which requires immediate action. BL

quackupuncture *n.* (quack + acupuncture) Misleading or fraudulent claims regarding the benefits of acupuncture. BNE

quaggy *adj.* (boggy + quagmire) Marshy; like a bog. TGP

Qualitone *brand name* Hearing aids, Qualitone. BTC

querious *adj.* (query + curious) Inquisitive; curious. BL

Questar *brand name* Telescopes, Questar Corp. BTC

queutopia *n.* (queue + utopia) A society in which shortages of material goods are chronic, and where inhabitants are forced to stand in line to acquire even the most basic necessities of life. Coined by Winston Churchill to describe what he imagined would be the ultimate result of a completely socialist economy. SEL

Quickonnect *brand name* Camera lock and release connector, Sima Products. BTC

Quiclip *brand name* Clips, Cableways Co., Inc. BTC

Quietone *brand name* Acoustical tile, United States Gypsum Co. BTC

Racerase *brand name* Erasable bond paper, Southworth Co. BTC

racon *n.* (radar + beacon) A radar beacon. DNW

racontage *n.* (raconteur + anecdotage) Skill in the art of telling anecdotes in a boisterous, entertaining manner. BNE

Radarange *brand name* Microwave ovens, Amana Refrigeration, Inc. BTC

radicalesbian *n.* (radical + lesbian) A lesbian with radical political views, especially regarding the rights of homosexuals. JO

radiodor *n.* (radio + odor) A disparaging label for a radio announcer, coined by Walter Winchell. AL

radiorator *n.* (radio + orator) One who regularly delivers public addresses on the radio. AL

radome *n.* (radar + dome) A dome-shaped housing that serves as a protective covering for radar equipment. BNW

Rainbowall *brand name* Information display boards, Trans-Lux Corp. BTC

Raisinuts *brand name* Snack foods, National Raisin Co. BTC

rampallion *n.* (ramp + rapscallion) A scoundrel or scamp. BPF

randem *adv.* (random + tandem) With three horses harnessed one behind the other, as in a carriage or wagon harness. WE

Randlord *n.* (Rand + landlord) An owner or manager of a gold field in the Rand, a gold-rich area of the Transvaal in South Africa. OED

rantankerous *adj.* (rancorous + cantankerous) Nineteenth century American slang, meaning bad-tempered, contentious or quarrelsome. AET

rapidry *adj.* (rapid + dry) Advertising coinage describing something which dries quickly. BAI

rasperated *adj.* (rasp + exasperated) Exasperated; irritated. BL

Ratstaurant *brand name* Rodenticide, Liphatech, Inc. BTC

Reaganomics *n.* (Reagan + economics) The national economic policies instituted during the administration of President Ronald Reagan.

Realemon *brand name* Lemon juice concentrate, ReaLemon Foods. BTC

Realime *brand name* Lime juice, ReaLemon Foods. BTC

rebuse *vb.* (rebuke + abuse) To harshly reprimand, from Shakespeare's *Taming of the Shrew.* BL

recomember *vb.* (recollect + remember) The act of remembering or reminiscing. Also: **recollember.** HDC BL

recouperation *n.* (recoup + recuperation) The act of recovering something or being compensated for that which has been lost. OED

rectenna *n.* (rectifying + antenna) An antenna which rectifies or converts microwave power to DC power. BNW

refujew *n.* (refugee + Jew) The colloquial name given to Jews who fled to the United States during the 1930s to escape Nazi persecution in Germany. DCS

Regallure *brand name* Fabric, Munsingwear, Inc. BTC

rendezwoo *n.* (rendezvous + woo) A meeting arranged between two lovers. BAI

replicar *n.* (replica + car) A full-size replica of a classic automobile which incorporates modern design features, and is typically delivered in pieces so that it can be assembled by the purchaser. BNE

repristination *n.* (reprise + restoration) The process of restoring something to its original condition. TGP

reprography *n.* (reproduction + photography) Photographic reproduction of original printed materials. BAI

Republocrat *n.* (Republican + Democrat) A Democratic Party member who often agrees with or supports Republicans; a Republican who favors Democratic Party policies; a political group made up of both Democrats and Republicans. Also: **Repulicrat.** WE, DNW, OED

Resistear *brand name* Sheet protectors, Stationers Guild of America. BTC

reversicon *n.* (reverse + lexicon) A dictionary organized in reverse fashion, listing word definitions as entries. MBD

revudeville *n.* (revue + vaudeville) A form of stage entertainment that combines elements of a musical revue and a vaudeville show. OED

revusical *n.* (revue + musical) A musical review. Coined by Walter Winchell. AL

riffle *n.* (ripple + ruffle) A segment of a river where the water flows swiftly and the water's surface is broken in small rippling waves. WE

rimbellisher *n.* (rim + embellisher) An ornamental chrome-plated trim ring that fits around the wheel hub of a motor vehicle. OED

ringoal *n.* (ring + goal) A game in which a hoop or ring is tossed at a goal by means of two sticks. OED

ritzycratic *adj.* (ritzy + aristocratic) High-toned, elegant, or luxurious. PBW

roadeo *n.* (road + rodeo) A contest involving a series of events intended to test the skills of motor vehicle drivers. WE

roaratorious *adj.* (roar + uproarious + notorious) Jubilantly boisterous. DS

roblitz *n.* (robot + blitz) An aerial attack by pilotless flying bombs, coined during World War II to describe V-1 rocket attacks on England. DNW

robomb *n.* (robot + bomb) A robot bomb; a name given to the pilotless V-1 rockets used by Germany during World War II. MBD

rockabilly *n.* (rock and roll + hillbilly) A form of popular music originating in the Southeastern United States, incorporating elements of rock and roll and hillbilly music. OED

rockappella *n.* (rock + a cappella) Rock music that features human voices without instrumental accompaniment.

rockoon *n.* (rocket + balloon) A balloon used to launch a research rocket from high altitudes. BNW

Rockoustics *brand name* Loudspeakers, GNP Audio/Video/Components. BTC

rockumentary *n.* (rock + documentary) A feature-length film made up of concert performances by rock musicians. NWD

roleo *n.* (roll + rodeo) A logrolling tournament. Also spelled **rolleo**. WE

rollick *vb.* (romp + frolic) To move about or behave in a carefree, joyous manner. WE

Romiette (Romeo + Juliet) A contraction of the title of Shakespeare's play *Romeo and Juliet.* AL

Rooflex *brand name* Roof coating, Sinclair Paint Co. BTC

Roomaker *brand name* Porch enclosure system, Continental Aluminum Products Co. BTC

Roomance *brand name* Air freshener, DeMert & Dougherty, Inc. BTC

rotovator *n.* (rotary + cultivator) A power-driven cultivator with rotating blades, designed for use in breaking up soil in gardens. BAR

Roundominoes *brand name* Strategy games and puzzles, Kadon Enterprises. BTC

routinary *adj.* (routine + ordinary) Of a commonplace, ordinary or repetitious character. OED

Royalight *brand name* Window blinds, shades and shutters, The Blindsman, Inc. BTC

rubbage *n.* (rubbish + garbage) Refuse; waste. TW

ruckus *n.* (ruction + rumpus) A noisy fight; a fracas. DWP

ruddervator *n.* (rudder + elevator) A movable airfoil on an airplane which performs the functions of a rudder and an elevator. WE

rumbumptious *adj.* (rumbustious + bump) Noisy and unruly. DS

rumbustious *adj.* (rumble + robustious) Rambunctious. WE

rumfle *vb.* (rumple + ruffle) To tousle or ruffle; to cause to be disheveled. BL

rumption *n.* (rumpus + gumption) A noisy or violent disturbance. DS

runagade *n.* (runner + renegade) In football, a fast, elusive running back. BAI

rurban *adj.* (rural + urban) Pertaining to a neighborhood or tract of land located within the boundaries of a city, but still retaining some of the characteristics of a rural area. DNW

Rustripper *brand name* Rust remover, Oakite Products, Inc. BTC

saccharhinoceros *n.* (saccharine + rhinoceros) A lumbering, oafish person who acts in an affectedly effusive or sentimental manner. OED

sacerdotage *n.* (sacerdotal + dotage) In religious doctrine, an over-emphasis on the power of priests, a tendency usually seen as a characteristic of a religion in decline. OED

saketini *n.* (sake + martini) A martini in which sake takes the place of vermouth. BG

salariat *n.* (salary + proletariat) The salaried workers within a work force, as distinguished from hourly wage earners. WE

saloonatic *n.* (saloon + lunatic) One who tends to act foolishly or irrationally while under the influence of alcohol. DA

samink *n.* (sable + mink) Mink fur produced through genetic mutation, and which is similar in appearance to Russian sable. BAR

sanctanimity *n.* (sanctimonious + magnanimity) Holiness. BL

sanctimoody *adj.* (sanctimonious + moody) Piously morose in demeanor. DS

Sandimals *brand name* Sandcast sculptures, Bandanna. BTC

Sandune *brand name* Ceramic tile, International American Ceramics, Inc. BTC

sandust *n.* (sand + dust) A pastel earth tint, somewhat yellowish-pink in color. WE

satelloon *n.* (satellite + balloon) A satellite launched from a high-altitude balloon. ID

satisfice *vb.* (satisfy + suffice) To set as a goal the minimum satisfactory condition or outcome. WES

Saturock *brand name* Asphaltic concrete mix, Carter-Waters Corp. BTC

saucerer *n.* (sorcerer + saucer) An individual who believes that UFOs can be summoned to appear by utilizing certain displays of lights, transmissions of radio beacons, or other means; a UFO enthusiast. TM

savagerous *adj.* (savage + dangerous) That which is ferocious, wild, violent and dangerous. AET

scamble *vb.* (scamper + scramble) The act of struggling with others for largesse thrown into a crowd. WE

scance *vb.* (scan + glance) To glance at or scan. BL

scandiculous *adj.* (scandalous + ridiculous) Outrageously scandalous. BL

Scandiknavery *n.* (Scandinavian + knavery) Trickery or deceit as practiced by Scandinavians. OED

scapathy *n.* (Scapa + apathy) British military slang for the mental depression servicemen suffer during long tours of duty in the Orkney Islands in northern Scotland, site of the Scapa Flow naval base. DS

scarify *vb.* (scare + terrify) To fill with terror. OED

Scentiments *brand name* Potpourri, Applewood Seed Co. BTC

Scentry *brand name* Fuel vapor detection system, Rule Industries, Inc. BTC

Scentsation *brand name* Air freshener, Blue Cross Laboratories. BTC

schooligan *n.* (school + hooligan) A student who exhibits disruptive behavior while in school. DA

scientifiction *n.* (scientific + fiction) Science fiction. WE

scissorean *n.* (scissor + Caesarean) Theft accomplished by cutting pages from a book. DS

scollage *n.* (scholar + college) College; a university education. BL

scooch *n.* (scotch + hooch) Intoxicating liquor. DS

Scowegian *n.* (Scandinavian + Norwegian) A colloquial name for a person from Scandinavia. DS

scrapnel *n.* (scrap + shrapnel) Metal fragments from a homemade bomb which has been filled with scrap metal for a more lethal effect. BNE

scrawl *vb., n.* (scribble + sprawl) Awkward, irregular writing or drawing; the act of producing such writings or drawings. WE

scraze *vb.* (scratch + graze) To scratch, scrape or graze. OED

Screwge *brand name* Light bulb and power saver, Miracle Products, Inc. BTC

screwmatics *n.* (screw + rheumatics) A colloquial name for rheumatism, derived from "The Screws," also slang for rheumatism. OED

scriggle *vb.* (squirm + wriggle) To wriggle or twist. WE

scringe *vb.* (shrink + cringe) To draw back or cower in fear. AET

scringe *n.* (syringe + cringe) A hypodermic syringe, a name derived from the typical reaction of patients about to be injected with one. FW

Scriptip *brand name* Markers, Scripto Tokai. BTC

scrolloping *n.* (scroll + lollop) Decoration characterized by the use of heavy, florid ornament. Coined by Virginia Woolf. OED

scrowsy *adj.* (screwy + lousy) That which is worthless, useless or contemptible. DAS

scrumble *vb.* (scrape + crumble) To scrape; to scratch out of or from. OED

scrump *vb.* (scratch + rumple) To playfully scratch or run fingers through one's own hair, or the hair of another. OE

scrumple *vb.* (squeeze + crumple) The act of crushing or squeezing. PBW

scrunch *vb.* (squeeze + crunch) To squeeze or crush. WE

Scrunge *brand name* Scrubber sponge, Church & Dwight Co. BTC

scrutineer *n.* (scrutiny + engineer) An official charged with the task of inspecting racing cars or other motorized vehicles to insure that they comply with regulations. OED

Scrutineyes *brand name* Optical products, Martin-Copland Co. BTC

scurb *n.* (skate + curb) A skateboarder. BL

scutter *vb.* (scatter + scuttle) To scurry or scuttle. WE

scuttle *vb.* (scud + shuttle) To move with short, rapid, alternating steps. WE

scuzzy *adj.* (scummy + lousy) Low, despicable, or slovenly. BNE

seafari *n.* (sea + safari) A journey involving travel by sea, particularly if undertaken for sport or recreation. OWW

Sealastic *brand name* Caulk and cork insulated tape, DeVan Sealants, Inc. BTC

seaquarium *n.* (sea + aquarium) A public aquarium; an aquarium specializing in the display of large marine animals. OED

Seaquarius *brand name* Powerboat, SeaCraft, Inc. BTC

seatron *n.* (sea + citron) A confection or conserve made from bladder kelp. WE

seavacuation *n.* (sea + evacuation) Evacuation to another location across the sea, first used to describe the evacuation of children from England to North America during World War II. LWW

seep *n.* (sea + jeep) A jeep that has been modified so it can operate in water. DNW

Seequence *brand name* Disposable contact lenses, Bausch & Lomb, Inc. BTC

sejole *vb.* (seduce + cajole) To lead astray by means of flattery. FW

selectorate *n.* (select + electorate) That segment of a political group which possesses the effective power to choose a representative. OED

Selectric *brand name* Electric typewriter, IBM Corporate Headquarters. BTC

Selectrim *brand name* Trimming system for boats, Outboard Marine Corp. BTC

Selectronic *brand name* Sewing machines, VWS, Inc. BTC

Senegambia *n.* (Senegal + Gambia) The former name of the region adjacent to the Senegal and Gambia rivers in Western Africa. OED

sennight *n.* (seven + night) A period of seven days and nights, or half the length of a *fortnight.* DWP

sensistor *n.* (sensor + resistor) A silicon resistor which senses variations in temperature, power, and time, and adjusts the electrical resistance accordingly. DST

sensorship *n.* (sensor + censorship) The department within a business or government agency responsible for collating results of polls and surveys. JA

Sensurround (sense + surround) Trademark for a cinematic sound system utilizing low-frequency sounds that the audience feels as subtle vibrations, an effect that is meant to enhance the impact of what is being shown on the screen. BNE

Serenitea *brand name* Herbal tea, Unitea Herbs.

sexational *adj.* (sex + sensational) Sexually startling or exciting. OED

sexcapade *n.* (sex + escapade) A sexual adventure. OED

Sexciting *brand name* Greeting cards, Kalan, Inc. BTC

sexclusive *adj.* (sex + exclusive) Pertaining to exclusive membership in any organization catering to the erotically inclined. DD

sexercise *n.* (sex + exercise) Sexual activity considered as a legitimate form of physical exercise; physical exercises which are promoted as a means of enhancing sexual performance; a euphemism for sexual activity. WW

sexetary *n.* (sex + secretary) A secretary whose job responsibilities include the dispensing of sexual favors. WW

sexhibition *n.* (sex + exhibition) A public display or performance that is conspicuously sexual in nature. DA

sexophone *n.* (sex + saxophone) The saxophone, an instrument often used in jazz compositions to express a brooding or sultry sense of mood; any musical instrument which is presumed to be capable of producing sexually stimulating sensations. OED

sexpert *n.* (sex + expert) A therapist who specializes in treating sexual problems. DAS

sexplanatory *adj.* (sex + explanatory) Pertaining to an explanation which is sexual in nature. DA

sexplicit *adj.* (sex + explicit) Sexually explicit. DA

sexploitation *n.* (sex + exploitation) An emphasis on provocative sexual content in order to attract a larger audience. DD

sexplosion *n.* (sex + explosion) A dramatic increase in the prevalence of pornographic and sexually explicit materials. DD

sexport *n.* (sex + export) A sexually alluring actress from a foreign country. DD

sexpose *n.* (sex + expose) An expose involving sexual misconduct. TM

sexpurgate *vb.* (sex + expurgate) To delete materials which might be considered obscene. TM

sextrovert *n.* (sex + extrovert) One who is willing to openly discuss personal interests or attitudes in regard to sexual behavior. TM

Shaconian *n.* (Shakespearean + Baconian) An advocate of the theory that Sir Francis Bacon actually wrote the plays attributed to William Shakespeare. MBD

shagreen *n.* (shag + green) Untanned leather, treated so that it is covered with small round granulations and then dyed a bright color, usually green. WE

shakesperience *n.* (Shakespeare + experience) An advertising coinage promoting theatrical productions of Shakespeare as memorable experiences for the audience.

shamateurism *n.* (sham + amateurism) The practice of paying money to non-professional athletes, such payments being conducted clandestinely so as not to jeopardize an athlete's amateur status. DJ

shambolic *adj.* (shamble + diabolic) Chaotic, disorderly or undisciplined. OED

shamburger *n.* (sham + hamburger) A hamburger patty made from soy protein or some other meat substitute.

shampagne *n.* (sham + champagne) A drink made of pink lemonade, ginger ale, and mint. The taste is said to resemble that of champagne, although it contains no alcohol. BAI

Shampooch *brand name* Dog shampoo, Norris Laboratories. BTC

Shampure *brand name* Hair-care products, Aveda Corp. BTC

Shanghailander *n.* (Shanghai + Highlander or islander) A native or inhabitant of Shanghai. OED

Sharprint *brand name* Computer paper, Badger Paper Mills, Inc. BTC

shedonism *n.* (she + hedonism) The attitude or behavior of a self-indulgent female, particularly a feminist. TM

shemale *n.* (she + female) A female; a male transvestite. ND

shepherdress *n.* (shepherdess + dress) A simple, pastoral style of dress, such as a shepherdess might wear. BAI

shero *n.* (she + hero) A female hero; a female character exhibiting great strength, courage, and nobility.

shifferrobe *n.* (chiffonier + wardrobe) A piece of furniture incorporating the characteristics of both a chiffonier and a wardrobe, in that it is a free-standing, two-door wardrobe with drawers behind one door, and a space for hanging clothes behind the other. BD

shim *pron.* (she + him) A proposed gender-neutral pronoun, to be used interchangeably in place of either *she* or *he.*

Shinyl *brand name* Vinyl floor covering, Congoleum Corp. BTC

shitticism *n.* (shit + witticism) A scatological figure of speech. Coined by American poet Robert Frost. OED

shivereens *n.* (shiver + smithereens) Fragments or pieces. OED

shoat *n.* (sheep + goat) The hybrid of a sheep and a goat. BNW

shouse *n.* (shit + house) Australian slang, used when referring to a privy. OED

Showering *brand name* Bathroom telephones, Enterprex International Corp. BTC

Showeround *brand name* Shower stalls, Plaskolite, Inc. BTC

siabon *n.* (siamang + gibbon) The offspring of a siamang ape and a gibbon. BAR

siberbia *n.* (Siberia + suburbia) The suburbs, in the sense that suburban life depends on access to an automobile, with the lack of one creating a sense of isolation comparable to that of life in Siberia. ID

sicklemia *n.* (sickle [cell] + anemia) In pathology, a contraction for the name of the blood disease sickle-cell anemia. OED

silcott *n.* (silk + cotton) Cloth made from woven cotton fibers and then finished to resemble silk, a material used chiefly in feminine undergarments. OED

Silentone *brand name* Mufflers, AP Parts Co. BTC

silumin *n.* (silicon + aluminum) A casting alloy of aluminum containing approximately 10 percent silicon. OED

simoleon *n.* (simon + napoleon) A dollar. *Simon* has been American slang for *dollar* since the early 19th century, while the *napoleon* is a French gold piece dating from about the same period. WE

sinclination *n.* (sin + inclination) A tendency or disposition towards sexual content or behavior.

sinema *n.* (sin + cinema) The pornographic movie industry. DA

Singlish *n.* (Singapore + English) The hybrid form of English commonly spoken in Singapore, combining words and phrases from the English, Chinese, Malay and Tamil languages. SE

singspiration *n.* (sing + inspiration) Songs of an intensely religious nature, as in a revival service. TGP

sinsational *adj.* (sin + sensation) Having the effect of arousing intense interest or excitement because of overt sexual content. TM

Sizzlean *brand name* Pork breakfast strips, Swift Eckrich. BTC

skatebordello *n.* (skateboard + bordello) A shop which caters to the material desires of skateboard enthusiasts. TM

skiddles *n.* (skid + skittles) A game in which sticks are thrown at pins of different point value which have been set up in a diamond pattern, also known as "stick bowling." WE

Skideck *brand name* Deck boat, Anchor Industries, Inc. BTC

skinjury *n.* (skin + injury) An advertising coinage that is used when referring to the treatment of minor cuts and abrasions. WWA

Skintillating *brand name* Bras and panties, Wacoal America, Inc. BTC

skish *n.* (skeet + fish) A target game for fishermen, in which a lead weight is cast at a target on the surface of the water or on the ground. WE

skitching *vb., n.* (ski + hitching) An informal winter activity popular among adolescents, performed by grasping a vehicle's bumper and maintaining one's balance in a crouching position as the vehicle drives across snow-covered pavement, pulling the sliding person along behind. WE

skitcom *n.* (skit + sitcom) Television comedy format in which the star appears in a series of unrelated comedy skits. SL

skort *n.* (short + skirt) A short skirt. ID

skurfing *n.* (skid + surfing) The sport of surfing on a coated plywood disc, first introduced in England in the 1950s. Also known as **skidboarding**. BNW

skyjack *vb.* (sky + hijack) To commandeer an airplane by force, usually for political motives. WE

skylon *n.* (sky + pylon) A tall, slim, graceful structure or sculpture, a word first applied to the spindle-shaped filigree spire erected on the south bank of the Thames during London's Festival of Britain in 1951. OED

slang *n.* (slovenly + language) Colloquial language which is not characteristic of conventional or standard usage. SSS

slanguage *n.* (slang + language) Slang, especially when considered as an integral component of everyday American speech. SE

slangular *adj.* (slang + angular) Having characteristics typical of slang. DS

slantindicular *adj.* (slant + perpendicular) Slanting on an angle from the perpendicular. DWP

slather *vb.* (slap + lather) To spread thickly or lavishly. WE

sleer *vb.* (slur + sneer) To sneer or mock. WE

slench *n.* (sluice + drench) A drenching splash of liquid. OE

slickery *n.* (slick + trickery) Unorthodox sports play, consisting of trickery and sleight of hand. BAI

slidder *vb.* (slither + slide) To glide with a slithering, sideways motion. OE

slightually *adj.* (slightly + actually) American slang, meaning "actually slightly." OED

Slimderella *brand name* Rubber girdles, Kleinert's, Inc. BTC

Slimmetry *brand name* Foundation garments, Formflex Foundations, Inc. BTC

Slimnastics *n.* (slim + gymnastics) A program of physical exercise, intended primarily as a way to help participants lose weight. WES

Slimplete *brand name* Nutritional supplements, Great Life Laboratories, Inc. BTC

slimpsy *adj.* (limp + slimsy) Lacking in substance or sturdiness; slimsy. WE

slimsy *adj.* (slim + flimsy) Flimsy or frail. WE

slithy *adj.* (slimy + lithe) Smooth and active; snakelike. Coined by Lewis Carroll. AA

slobgollion *n.* (slop + slumgullion) A slimy, stringy substance found in sperm whale oil. DS

sloburb *n.* (slob + suburb) An unsightly, poorly planned residential area on the outskirts of a city. BAI

sloosh *n.* (slush + sluice) A stream or cascade of water; the noise made by rushing water. OED

slopperati *n.* (sloppy + literati) A group of individuals who deliberately dress in a bedraggled manner because it is thought to be fashionable. NW

slosh *n., vb.* (slop + slush) Slush, a thick mixture of half-melted snow; to splash or move clumsily through water or mud. WE

slounge *vb.* (slouch + lounge) To lounge about in a relaxed or lazy manner. WE

slub *n.* (slum + suburb) A suburban area in which the quality of the housing is inferior and the living conditions substandard. BNW

slumpflation *n.* (slump + inflation) Stagnant economic conditions, characterized by rising rates of unemployment and inflation. Also known as **stagflation** or **inflump**. DJ

slurb *n.* (slum + suburbs) A suburb characterized by drearily uniform houses of poor construction, and unplanned or haphazard development. ND

slurch *n., vb.* (slink + lurch) Physical movement involving alternating gliding and lurching motions. BAI

smarm *vb.* (smear + balm) To smear with something greasy or sticky, from which **smarmy**, the tendency to flatter fulsomely, is derived. DS

smash *n., vb.* (smack + mash) A hard, heavy hit or blow; the act of striking a heavy blow. WE

smatchet *n.* (smash + hatchet) A large, heavy-bladed knife issued to Allied commandoes during World War II. OE

smaze *n.* (smoke + haze) Murky atmospheric conditions, caused by a combination of smoke and haze. TGP

smealth *n.* (smell + health) In medicine, the appraisal of an individual's body odors as one means of determining the state of that person's health.

smelodious *adj.* (smell + odious) That which is malignant or hateful. SEL

smeuse *n.* (smoot + meuse) British dialect word for an opening in a hedge or wall (meuse) which leads from one lane or passageway (smoot) to another. WE

smice *n.* (smoke + ice) An atmospheric condition which occurs when smoke mixes with precipitation in the form of ice granules. ID

smist *n.* (smoke + mist) A mixture of smoke and mist. FW

smog *n.* (smoke + fog) An atmospheric condition caused by a blend of fog, smoke and chemical fumes. The word was coined by the Public Health Congress in London in 1905, to describe that city's notoriously polluted air. DWP

smokolotive *n.* (smoke + locomotive) A locomotive. BL

smores *n.* (some + more) A candy treat made by topping a graham cracker with a chocolate bar and marshmallow, and then heating it. Famous as a traditional campfire treat of the Girl Scouts, **smores** represents a contracted form of the frequent request for "some more" of the candy. SSS

smorgasborgy *n.* (smorgasbord + orgy) An orgy distinguished by the variety of sexual practices indulged in by the participants. DA

Smorgasgrill *brand name* Glass cooker for hors d'oeuvres, The Holdings, Inc. BTC

smotheration *n.* (smother + suffocation) A state of smothering or being smothered. WE

smothercate *vb.* (smother + suffocate) To smother or stifle. BL

smoud *n.* (smoke + cloud) Murky atmospheric conditions caused by a combination of smoke and clouds. SOL

smurk *n.* (smoke + murk) Dirty, polluted air. DNW

smust *n.* (smoke + dust) Atmospheric haze created by a combination of smoke and dust. SEL

snain *n.* (snow + rain) Snow and rain mixed; freezing rain. TGP

snangle *vb.* (snarl + tangle) To snarl or tangle. BL

snark *n.* (snake + shark) An imaginary creature, the quest for which is the basis of Lewis Carroll's poem *The Hunting of the Snark.* DWP

snazzy *adj.* (snappy + jazzy) That which is smart and fashionable. DCS

sneakret *n.* (sneak + secret) A secret. BL

sneet *n.* (snow + sleet) Precipitation which is a combination of snow and sleet. TGP

snicker *vb., n.* (snigger + nicker) To laugh in a suppressed, stifled, insinuating manner. OED

snirt *n.* (snow + dirt) Old snow with the dirt showing through. FW

snitter *vb.* (snicker or snigger + titter) To laugh in a suppressed, nervous manner. OED

snitzy *adj.* (snazzy + ritzy) That which is luxurious or elegant. ND

snivelization *n.* (snivel + civilization) A derisive label for modern society, perceived as a source of anxiety and moral weakness. Coined by American author Herman Melville in his novel *Redburn.* OED

snob *n.* (snip + cobbler) British dialect word for a shoemaker or cobbler. WE

snobject *n.* (snob + object) An object which has snob appeal because of its cost or scarcity. BAI

snoblem *n.* (snob + problem) The esoteric concern of a small, elitist group. BAI

snofari *n.* (snow + safari) A hunting expedition into snow-covered territory; a colloquial term for a group skiing vacation. OWW

snoopervise *vb.* (snoop + supervise) To supervise by means of prying interference. Also: **snoopervision.** HDC

snoozle *vb.* (snooze + nuzzle) To nestle comfortably and then fall asleep. DS

snoud *n.* (snow + cloud) An atmospheric condition created by snow and low clouds. FW

Snowolf *brand name* Snowthrowers, MTD Products, Inc. BTC

snurfing *n.* (snow + surfing) A variation on the sport of snow skiing, in which a specially designed plastic board similar to a surfboard takes the place of snow skis. BNE

snuzzle *vb.* (snug + nuzzle) To nestle or snuggle. WE

soaperatic *adj.* (soap + operatic) Exhibiting the characteristics of a soap opera. SEL

Socialights *brand name* Glass candles, Anchor Hocking Corp. BTC

Socketool *brand name* Socket sets, Green Duck Co. BTC

sodar *n.* (sound + radar) A technique for investigating conditions of the upper atmosphere, similar in principle to radar, but utilizing ultrasonic waves instead of microwaves. OED

Softalk *brand name* Telephone shoulder rests, Softalk, Inc. BTC

Softan *brand name* Leather cases, Korchmar Leather Specialty Co. BTC

Softint *brand name* Hair coloring, Revlon, Inc. BTC

Softip *brand name* Paintbrushes, The Wooster Brush Co. BTC

Softouch *brand name* Napkins, Textol Co., Inc. BTC

Softoys *brand name* Plush toys, Coronet Toy Mfg. Co., Inc. BTC

Softread *brand name* Mats, Cactus Mat Mfg. Co. BTC

sojourney *vb.* (sojourn + journey) To travel. OED

Solaroom *brand name* Sunrooms, Janco Greenhouses. BTC

solemncholy *adj.* (solemn + melancholy) Relentlessly and depressingly somber in demeanor. DS

soliloquacity *n.* (soliloquy + loquacity) A tendency to indulge in lengthy soliloquies. BAI

soliloquery *n.* (soliloquy + query) A lengthy, one-sided inquiry. TM

soliquid *n.* (solid + liquid) A liquid in which solid particles are dispersed or suspended. DST

solunar *adj.* (solar + lunar) Resulting from the combined actions of the sun and moon. WE

somniloquacious *adj.* (somniloquent + loquacious) Subject to a tendency to talk in one's sleep. MBD

somnorific *adj.* (somnific + soporific) Somniferous; likely to induce sleep. WE

Sophisticrepe *brand name* Decorative streamers and rolls, Cindus Corp. BTC

sorernity *n.* (sorority + fraternity) Campus student housing admitting both male and female students, also known as a **fratority**. DA

soroptimist *n.* (sorority + optimist) A member of a service club composed primarily of professional women. WE

sothers *n.* (sisters + brothers) A group of sisters and brothers. AL

Soundesign *brand name* Audio and video equipment and accessories, Soundesign Corp. BTC

soundscape *n.* (sound + landscape) The representation of an idea or image in sound, consisting of music, nonmusical sounds, or both. WES

Sovietnam *n.* (Soviet + Vietnam) A name applied to the Soviet invasion and occupation of Afghanistan, implying that the failure of that Soviet military campaign parallels the American experience in Vietnam.

Soygurt *brand name* Nondairy yogurt, Cream of the Beam, Inc. BTC

Spanglish *n.* (Spanish + English) A hybrid form of Spanish and English which is commonly used in ethnic Spanish neighborhoods such as those in Miami, Los Angeles, and New York. WES

spansule *n.* (span + capsule) A timed or time-release capsule, designed to release specific doses of medication within a certain time span. BNW

sparcity *n.* (sparse + scarcity) A condition of acute scarcity. DWP

Sparklens *brand name* Optical products, Benson Optical Co., Inc. BTC

specialogue *n.* (special + catalog) A merchandising catalog which is aimed at a specific market. NW

spendacious *adj.* (spend + mendacious) Pertaining to government agencies which use portions of their budgets for wasteful or fraudulent purposes. DA

spetch *n.* (speck + patch) Scraps and bits of refuse trimmed from leather, hides or skins. WE

Spinnish *n.* (spin + Spanish) Purportedly neutral language which is actually intended to manipulate, slant or alter the public's perception of events. The use of "spin" to describe such manipulative versions of events derives from the spin or "English" applied to a billiard ball or other moving object. AM

Spinsect *brand name* Insect traps, Ampsco Corp. BTC

Spinsulation *brand name* Fiberglass insulation, Manville Fiber Glass Group. BTC

Spinut *brand name* Spinner ratchets, Davenport Tool Co. BTC

splake *n.* (speckled trout + lake trout) A hybrid of the American lake trout and the brook trout. WE

splanch *n.* (split-level + ranch) A house combining features of a ranch-style home with those of a split-level design. BNE

splather *vb.* (splash + blather) To spread rumors or misinformation in a confusing manner. WE

splatter *vb.* (splash + spatter) To spatter or splash. WE

splork *n.* (split + fork) A variety of pitch in baseball, in which the pitcher's splay-fingered grip on the ball, like that used in the split-fingered fastball, creates movement of the ball in flight similar to that of a forkball.

splosh *vb.* (splash + slosh) To splash or make a splashing sound. OED

splotch *n.* (spot + blotch) A contrasting daub or smear, usually occurring as the result of accidental spillage. WE

splunge *vb.* (splash + plunge) The act of plunging into water. WE

splurge *n., vb.* (splash + surge) An ostentatious or conspicuous demonstration or effort; to act in such a manner. WE

splutter *n., vb.* (splash + sputter) A confused noise; a violent splashing or sputtering. WE

Spock-marked *adj.* (Spock + pock-marked) Pertaining to a spoiled or self-indulgent child, presumed to be the result of the permissive parenting encouraged by Dr. Benjamin Spock, American physician and author of several popular child care books. OED

Spoodle *brand name* Serving ladles, The Vollrath Co. BTC

spork *n.* (spoon + fork) A spoon, usually made of plastic, which has several blunt tines so that it can also be used as a fork. BNE

Sportea *brand name* Beverage, Ultimate Performance Products, Inc. BTC

Sportimers *brand name* Watches, LeMans Time Corp. BTC

Sportote *brand name* Tote bag, Davy Products, Inc. BTC

Sportours *brand name* Travel programs, Travel Mates International, Inc. BTC

sposh *n.* (slush + posh) An American dialect word for soft, slushy mud or snow, **posh** being an archaic word for slush or mud. AET

Spotone *brand name* Photographic retouching solution, Retouch Methods Co., Inc. BTC

sprinter *n.* (spring + winter) A period of unseasonably cold weather in the late spring, or unusually warm and spring-like weather in mid-winter. MBN

squabash *vb.* (squash + bash) To crush or beat down with vitriolic criticism. WE

squadrilla *n.* (squadron + flotilla) A word invented during World War I to describe a squadron of airplanes. OED

squadrol *n.* (squad + patrol) A small van used by police as both a squad car and ambulance. WE

squalmish *adj.* (squeamish + qualm) Squeamish. BL

squanderlust *n.* (squander + wanderlust) An overwhelming urge to spend all of one's financial assets. OED

squarson *n.* (squire + parson) A clergyman who is also a landlord; a clergyman who uses church funds to improve or purchase property for his own use. MBD

squash *vb.* (squeeze + crash) To press or crush completely. SEL

squattage *n.* (squatter + cottage) Australian slang for a squatter's homestead. DS

squdgy *adj.* (squat + pudgy) Squat and pudgy. WE

squench *vb.* (quench + squelch) To extinguish. BL

squiggle *vb.* (squirm + wriggle) To squirm or wriggle. WE

squinch *vb.* (squint + pinch) To squint one's eyes, or in some other manner contort one's face. WE

squirk *n.* (squirm + twirl) A flourish or twist. WE

squirl *n.* (squiggle + whirl or twirl) A twirl or flourish, especially as a characteristic of an expressive style of handwriting. OED

squish *vb.* (squirt + squash) To squash or squelch. WE

squishop *n.* (squire + bishop) A bishop who is also a landlord, or an owner of extensive property. Also: **squarson.** YNW

squiz *n.* (squint + quiz) Australian slang, meaning a quick look or glance. OED

squnch *vb.* (squeeze + crunch) To squeeze into a small area. BL

squoggy *adj.* (soggy + quaggy) Wet; characteristic of a mire or bog. OED

stabilator *n.* (stabilizer + elevator) A movable, horizontal section on the tail of an airplane, used to control its direction in flight. DST

stabile *n.* (stable + mobile) A rigid sculpture that is typically constructed of metal pipes, bars, sheet metal or similar materials. Developed by artist Alexander Calder, master of the kinetic mobile, and named by artist Jean Arp. OED

stagflation *n.* (stagnation + inflation) A period of economic malaise characterized by growing unemployment and a rising rate of inflation. DJ

Standastic *brand name* Musical keyboard and computer stands, Standastic. BTC

stanine *n.* (standard [score] + nine) An aptitude score used in the testing of aviation students, typically ranging from a score of one to nine. WE

Starider *brand name* Bicycles, Ross Bicycles, Inc. BTC

Statemints *brand name* Candy, Statemints. BTC

stator *n.* (stationary + rotor) A stationary machine part in or about which a rotor turns. DST

Steamarvel *brand name* Steamer basket insert, Vita-Saver, Inc. BTC

steelionaire *n.* (steel + millionaire) A millionaire whose wealth stems from investments in the steel industry. WWA

stellarator *n.* (stellar + generator) A device that applies magnetic forces to plasma gas confined in a sealed tube to produce thermonuclear power, a process of generating energy similar to that which is believed to occur in stars. BAR

stencilhouette *n.* (stencil + silhouette) A silhouette done in stencil. BL

stewp *n.* (stew + soup) A mixture of food which is too thick to be called soup, and too thin to be stew. FW

stiction *n.* (static + friction) Static friction. OED

Stipplease *brand name* Paints, Perfection Paint & Color Co. BTC

stockateer *n.* (stock + racketeer) A broker dealing in fraudulent securities. WE

Storack *brand name* Adjustable storage bins and racks, Frick-Gallagher Mfg. Co. BTC

stramp *vb.* (stamp + tramp) To trample. WE

striggle *n.* (straggle + wiggle) A wavy line. OED

stringlet *n.* (string + ringlet) A ringlet. BL

stripteuse *n.* (stripper + chanteuse) A striptease artist who sings while she removes her clothing. WWA

strome *vb.* (stroll + roam) To stride or stroll. WE

Stronglaze *brand name* Thread, United Thread Mills Corp. BTC

studdle *vb.* (stir + muddle) To make water muddy by stirring it up; to roil. WE

stuffocation *n.* (stuff + suffocation) A condition brought on by overeating, to the extent that a person finds it virtually impossible to breathe.

stultiloquence *n.* (stultified + eloquence) Foolish or senseless talk. YNW

Stylast *brand name* Hair-setting product, Dow Brands. BTC

Styleader's *brand name* Footwear, Berle Shoe Co. BTC

Styledge *brand name* Beauty aids, Dubl Duck/Jet Set, Inc. BTC

subtopia *n.* (suburban + utopia) An ironic term of disparagement, used to describe areas of poorly planned suburban development; well-planned suburban communities that represent ideal places in which to live. OED

Sugaripe *brand name* Raisins, Dole Dried Fruit & Nut Co. BTC

Sunsitive *brand name* Sun-protection products, Tanning Research Laboratories, Inc. BTC

Superamics *brand name* Kilns, Superamics. BTC

Superase *brand name* Bond paper, Gilbert Paper Co. BTC

superfecta *n.* (super + perfecta) A variation on perfecta race betting in which the object is to pick all four winners in their correct order of finish. WES

Superoof *brand name* Fiberglass roof panels, Dyrotech Industries, Inc. BTC

Supremium *brand name* Gasoline, Ashland Oil, Inc. BTC

surfactant *n.* (surface + active + agent) A soluble compound that reduces the surface tension of liquids. DST

surfari *n.* (surf + safari) An expedition of surfers intent on searching for optimum conditions in which to go surfing. OWW

surficial *adj.* (surface + superficial) Of or relating to a surface, often used to refer to the surface of the earth. WE

surroundry *n.* (surround + boundary) An encompassing boundary. OED

suspose *vb.* (suspect + suppose) To suppose or imagine. BL

swacket *n.* (sweater + jacket) A heavy sweater that can be buttoned like a jacket. BAI

swallet *n.* (swallow + gullet) An underground stream such as those often encountered by miners; the opening through which a stream disappears underground. OED

swash *n., vb.* (splash + swagger) A body or mass of dashing, splashing water; to act in a blustering or bullying manner. AHD

sweatspiration *n.* (sweat + perspiration) Perspiration. BL

sweedle *vb.* (swindle + wheedle) To commit a swindle by wheedling. OED

Sweetarts *brand name* Candy, Sunline Brands. BTC

Sweetaste *brand name* Artificial sweetener, Purepac Pharmaceutical Co. BTC

Sweetreat *brand name* Candy, R. M. Palmer Co. BTC

Sweetrim *brand name* No-calorie sweetener, Billings & Gage Mfg. Co. BTC

swelegant *adj.* (swell + elegant) Self-consciously elegant. Coined by Walter Winchell. WW

swelp *n.* (so + help) A perennial complainer, originating from the phrase "So help me God..." MBD

sweltry *adj.* (swelter + sultry) Oppressively hot. OED

swilge *n.* (swill + bilge) A weak and thoroughly unappetizing concoction of instant coffee. DS

Swimaster *brand name* Swimming and skin-diving equipment, Voit Sports, Inc. BTC

swingle *n.* (single + swing) A single person who leads a fashionable, frenetic, and often promiscuous lifestyle; a single person in search of a sexual partner. DAS

Swinglish *n.* (Swedish + English) English words and phrases which have been adapted as part of the Swedish language. SE

swipe *n., vb.* (wipe + sweep) To cut, strike or hit with a sweeping motion; the act of striking in such a manner. WE

swizzle *vb.* (swill + guzzle) To guzzle or imbibe noisily. BL

swoose *n.* (swan + goose) A hybrid resulting from the mating of a swan with a goose. The plural form is **sweese**. WE

symbolatry *n.* (symbol + idolatry) The worship or excessive veneration of symbols. OED

systemaniac *n.* (system + maniac) A person who insists on rigidly adhering to systematic methods, no matter how tedious or impractical. TM

taboobery *n.* (taboo + boob) Extremism in defense of rigid moral standards; an exaggerated sense of moral righteousness. Coined by American sociologist Franklin H. Giddings. AL

taileron *n.* (tail + aileron) A horizontal control surface mounted on the tail of an airplane which functions as an elevator and an aileron. OED

tamboo *n.* (tambour + bamboo) A small West Indies drum made from bamboo. OED

tangelo *n.* (tangerine + pomelo) A hybrid of the tangerine and pomelo, resulting in a citrus fruit similar to a grapefruit or a large, thick-skinned orange. FO

tangemon *n.* (tangerine + lemon) A hybrid of the tangerine and lemon. WE

tangor *n.* (tangerine + orange) A hybrid of the mandarin orange and sweet orange, popular because it is easy to peel and has a distinctive, aromatic flavor. WE

Tantaleyes *brand name* Optical products, Welling International. BTC

Tanzania *n.* (Tanganyika + Zanzibar) A country in eastern Africa, made up of the countries of Tanganyika and Zanzibar, which united in 1964. The new country's name of Tanzania was adopted after "The United Republic of Tanganyika and Zanzibar" proved impractical for everyday use.

Taperaser *brand name* Typing correction material, Dixon Ticonderoga Co. BTC

tarnation *adv., adj.* (tarnal + damnation) A euphemistic oath, meaning the same as "damnation." WE

Teabaco *brand name* Snuff, Earth Harvest. BTC

Teasoning *brand name* Seasonings, House of Herbs, Inc. BTC

telecommuter *n.* (telecommunications + commuter) An employee whose home workplace is connected to his employer via a computer modem or some other element of a telecommunications network. BAR

telectorate *n.* (television + electorate) That portion of a television audience which is eligible to vote. BDC

telegogue *n.* (television + demagogue) A person with the power to select and edit the features to be shown in television news programs. WW

telephonetics *n.* (telephone + phonetics) The practice of using a phone; the act of signalling through the use of sounds. OED

telephonograph *n.* (telephone + phonograph) An instrument developed in the 1880s that functioned as a rudimentary answering machine, in that it could be used to record telephone messages and play them back. OED

televangelist *n.* (television + evangelist) A religious leader who attempts to convince people to join or support a particular church or religious belief by means of televised sermons.

televisionary *n.* (television + visionary) A person who shows unusual foresight in developing programming for television; a television enthusiast; a television personality. DA

tenigue *n.* (tension + fatigue) Physical and mental exhaustion brought on by psychological strain and a lack of physical exercise. DNW

tenoroon *n.* (tenor + bassoon) A wood reed instrument with a musical pitch between the oboe and the bassoon. OED

tensegrity *n.* (tension + integrity) The property of a structural framework combining continuous tension components such as wires, and discontinuous rigid members such as metal rods or tubes. The proper application of tensegrity can result in a stable, self-supporting form, such as that of a geodesic dome. WES

terraqueous *adj.* (terra + aqueous) Consisting of both land and water. WE

terrorilla *n.* (terrorist + guerrilla) A term used to describe the form of guerrilla warfare conducted against the Israeli military in southern Lebanon. NWD

testiculating *vb.* (testicles + gesticulating) Provocatively waving and gesturing while talking in a brazen manner. This colloquial term derives from the belief that behaving in this way in public "takes a lot of balls." DS

testificate *n.* (testimonial + certificate) Documentation which testifies to the qualities of a particular person or thing. BL

Texarkana *n.* (Texas + Arkansas + Louisiana) A city straddling the Texas-Arkansas border slightly north of Louisiana. The name is thought to have originated from the *Texarkana,* a famous 19th century steamboat which regularly traveled along the Red River, the current boundary between Texas and Arkansas. NOL

Texcentricity *n.* (Texas + eccentricity) The distinctively eccentric behavior exhibited by some natives of Texas; the condition of being overtly Texan. DD

Texican *n.* (Texan + Mexican) A Texan with a Mexican background. In the early 1800s, when Texas was still part of the Spanish territory of Mexico, settlers there called themselves Texicans to set themselves apart from Spanish-speaking Mexicans. OED

Texico *n.* (Texas + New Mexico) A town in New Mexico, just west of the border with Texas. AL

Theraffin *brand name* Parrafin wax for use in therapy, W. R. Medical Electronics Co. BTC

Thermalarm *brand name* Alarm, Rampart Corp. BTC

Thermassage *brand name* Massager, Elexis Corp. BTC

thermistor *n.* (thermal + resistor) An electrical resistor with a level of resistance which varies with the temperature. WE

Thindex *brand name* Folders, Esselte Pendaflex Corp. BTC

Thinsulate *brand name* Thermal insulation for apparel, 3M Co. BTC

thon *pron.* (that + one) A third-person, gender-neutral pronoun which can be used in place of either "he" or "she." Introduced in 1858 by American composer C. C. Converse.

thoughtography *n.* (thought + photography) A paranormal phenomenon in which visible photographic images are produced by concentrated mental effort. OED

threepeat *n.* (three + repeat) The repetition of a particular act or achievement three times in a row. Sometimes hyphenated as **three-peat**.

Thriftape *brand name* Tape, Le Page's, Inc. BTC

thrinter *n.* (three + winter) A three-year-old sheep. WE

thumble *vb.* (thunder + rumble) To rumble in a manner similar to thunder. OED

Thunderwear *brand name* Rainsuits, Thunderwear, Inc. BTC

thwack *vb., n.* (thump + whack) To strike a blow with something flat or heavy; a blow of this kind. WE

tigon *n.* (tiger + lion) A hybrid of a male tiger and a female lion. The tigon generally has large dark patches or bars for markings, similar to that of a clouded leopard. Other cat hybrids include the **tiglon** and **liger**. WE

tilge *n.* (tea + bilge) Brewed tea which has been allowed to become unpleasantly stale or tepid. BL

Timinder *brand name* Desk top reminder light, Timark. BTC

tinner *n.* (tea + dinner) British slang, indicating a meal which serves as both afternoon tea and dinner. DS

tipple *vb.* (tip + topple) To topple or tumble over. OED

tissue *n.* (trivial + issue) Political jargon for an issue of little real importance, but having potentially great emotional impact with voters. JA

tizzy *n.* (tipsy + dizzy) An excited, foolishly distracted or baffled state of mind. WE

tobaccoholic *n.* (tobacco + alcoholic) A person who exhibits a compulsive addiction to tobacco. BDC

tobacconalian *n.* (tobacco + bacchanalian) A person addicted to the pleasures of tobacco. OED

Tofait *brand name* Frozen tofu dessert products, Hawthorn Mellody, Inc. BTC

Tofoodles *brand name* Tofu noodles, CR Foods, Inc. BTC

topato *n.* (tomato + potato) A hybrid of the tomato and potato, also known as a **pomato**. WE

topepo *n.* (tomato + pepper) A hybrid of the tomato and sweet pepper. WE

torrible *adj.* (torrid + horrible) Terribly hot, normally used in describing hot weather. BL

tosh *n.* (toe + wash) A foot bath. BL

touron *n.* (tourist + moron) An annoyingly stupid tourist. SL

tove *n.* (turtle + dove) A turtle dove. Coined by Lewis Carroll. TW

toxicyst *n.* (toxic + cyst) A minute structure on the surface of a one-celled organism that can release toxic filaments which induce paralysis in the organism's prey. DST

trafficator *n.* (traffic + indicator) An early design for a motor vehicle directional signal, consisting of a pair of signal arms attached to the sides of a vehicle; either arm could be extended by the driver to indicate a turn. WE

tragicomedy *n.* (tragic + comedy) A drama combining elements of tragedy and comedy, with tragedy usually predominating. WE

trainasium *n.* (training + gymnasium) A gymnasium used by athletes exclusively for training. AEM

trampede *n., vb.* (trample + stampede) A stampede; the act of taking part in a stampede; to cause a stampede.

trampoose *vb.* (tramp + vamoose) To tramp or trudge. OED

Tranquilounger *brand name* Recliners, Lewittes Furniture Enterprises, Inc. BTC

transceiver *n.* (transmitter + receiver) A radio transmitter-receiver. WE

transescent *n.* (transition + adolescent) Educational jargon used in reference to a child attending junior high or middle school, and thus making the transition from elementary to high school.

transfection *n.* (transfer + infection) The process by which material is introduced into a living cell. OED

transistor *n.* (transfer + resistor) A miniaturized electronic device which controls the flow of current without employing a vacuum. WE

translute *vb.* (translate + convolute) An act of translation in which the original meaning of the translated work is completely altered. WO

transonic *adj.* (transitional + sonic) At a speed approximating the speed of sound. WE

transparesscent *adj.* (transparent + essence + scent) Advertising coinage describing the delicate, subtle effects of fine perfume. BAI

transponder *n.* (transmitter + responder) An electronic device carried on an aircraft which emits coded signals identifying the plane when triggered by a radar beam. WE

transputer *n.* (transistor + computer) A powerful computer chip incorporating all of the functions of a microprocessor, including memory. OED

transverter *n.* (transformer + converter) An apparatus which can be used to convert AC electrical current to DC current, and vice versa. OED

trantelope *n.* (tarantula + antelope) An Australian colloquial name for a tarantula, perhaps referring in an exaggerated way to the extraordinary speed and size of the Australian species. DS

travelator *n.* (travel + escalator) A horizontal moving walkway in an airport. BNW

Travelid *brand name* Lids for paper and plastic containers, Ft. Howard Corp. BTC

Travelodge *brand name* Hotel/motel chain, Trusthouse Forte Hotels International, Inc. BTC

travelogue *n.* (travel + monologue) A lecture on some aspect of travel. Coined by lecturer Burton Holmes during a speaking tour of London in 1904, so as not to repel the public with the imposing term **lecture.** AL

tremblor *n.* (temblor + trembler) An earth tremor. OED

tremense *adj.* (tremendous + immense) Unusually large. FW

trendency *n.* (trend + tendency) A trend towards a particular course of action or attitude. DA

trialevision *n.* (trial + television) Use of videotaped testimony in the courtroom. TM

triathlete *n.* (triathlon + athlete) An athlete who competes in a triathlon. WES

tricknology *n.* (trick + technology) Apparent technological advances which in fact give merely an illusion of progress. DA

triggernometry *n.* (trigger + trigonometry) Advertising coinage for the artistry of a marksman specializing in fast-draw demonstrations. DD

tripewriter *n.* (tripe + typewriter) A hack writer whose work is trivial, disreputable or offensive. DAS

tritical *adj.* (trite + critical) Of a trite nature. OED

triticale *n.* (Triticum + Secale) The name of a hybrid of wheat and rye, derived from the plant genera of each. **Triticale** was apparently chosen in preference to blended words using rye and wheat, which produced names including **whye** and **reat**. BDN

triumpherate *n.* (triumph + triumvirate) A triumvirate, an administrative arrangement in the government of ancient Rome in which three men shared equal powers. Used either ironically or erroneously by Shakespeare in *Antony and Cleopatra* and *Love's Labour's Lost*. BL

tromp *vb.* (tramp + stomp) To walk with a firm and heavy tread. AHD

Tropicolors *brand name* Nail polishes, Del Laboratories, Inc. BTC

Tropicool *brand name* Fruit drinks, Johanna Farms. BTC

troposcatter *n.* (troposphere + scatter) The tendency of radio waves to be scattered by clouds and particulate matter suspended in the atmosphere. OED

truppie *n.* (truck + yuppie) An upwardly mobile trucker who takes his spouse or family along on the road, providing living accommodations in an elongated cabin similar to a mobile home. NWD

Tudorbethan *n.* (Tudor + Elizabethan) Mock Tudor style; in a style imitative of the Tudor and Elizabethan periods. OED

tuftaffeta *n.* (tuft + taffeta) Fabric that is a variation of taffeta, with its pile arranged in tufts. WE

tumblesault *n.* (tumble + somersault) A somersault. DWP

tumoil *n.* (tumult + turmoil) A tumultuous, confused condition. PBW

turken *n.* (turkey + chicken, or turkey + hen) A variety of chicken that is characterized by a rough, red, unfeathered neck, somewhat resembling the wattle of a turkey. Also known as a **churkey**. WE

twee *adj.* (tiny + wee) A dialect word used in northern England to indicate that something is very small. BL

tweenager *n.* ('tween + teenager) An adolescent between the ages of childhood and puberty, typically between nine and twelve years old, also called a **betweenager**.

twiddle *vb., n.* (twirl + fiddle) The act of twirling or twisting something; a small change in a computer program, or the act of making such a change. DJ

twindle *vb.* (twist + dwindle) To twist freely in the air. Coined by the poet Gerard Manley Hopkins. OED

Twindow *brand name* Multiple glazed window units, PPG Industries. BTC

twinight *n.* (twilight + night) An interval of time including the hours of twilight and nighttime, used most often to describe baseball games which begin in the late afternoon and continue into the nighttime hours. WE

Twinjector *brand name* Razors and blades, The Gillette Co. BTC

twinsult *n.* (twin + insult) A double insult. TM

twinter *n.* (twin + winter) A sheep, ox or horse which has lived through two winters. An animal which has survived three winters is known as a **thrinter**. WE

twirl *vb.* (twist + whirl) To revolve rapidly. AHD

twirligig *n.* (twirl + whirligig) A twirled pattern; a whirligig. OED

Twistrap *brand name* Wire products, Mid-States Wire. BTC

twit *n.* (twerp + twat) A slang term of abuse, used to describe someone annoyingly ignorant or silly. DCS

ubiquinone *n.* (ubiquitous + quinone) A class of common crystalline compounds which act as electron-transfer agents in cell respiration. OED

ubookquitous *adj.* (ubiquitous + book) A book which seems to be promoted or offered for sale virtually everywhere at once. MBN

uffish *adj.* (uppish + selfish) Uppity; self-centered. Also used by Lewis Carroll to mean **grumpy**. FW

ufocal *n.* (UFO + focal) A locality which is considered an optimum site for encounters with UFOs. DJ

uforia *n.* (UFO + euphoria) Enthusiastic belief in the existence of unidentified flying objects; the title of a 1981 science fiction movie concerning flying saucer hysteria. MOT

Ulsteria *n.* (Ulster + hysteria) The impassioned and violent brand of politics practiced by the inhabitants of Ulster, a province of Northern Ireland. BL

Ultamints *brand name* Candy, Warner-Lambert Co. BTC

Ultime *brand name* Watches and clocks, Bulova Corp. BTC

ultraviolation *n.* (ultraviolet + violation) A humorous blend word denoting the process of irradiation with ultraviolet light. OED

Umbrellegant *brand name* Umbrellas, L. P. Henryson Co., Inc. BTC

Umbroller *brand name* Baby stroller, Graco Children's Products. BTC

umperor *n.* (umpire + emperor) An imperious umpire. BL

Uncle Tomahawk *n.* (Uncle Tom + tomahawk) A derisive name given to Indians who are accused of abandoning their heritage because they have embraced the values of white society. Similarly, "Uncle Tom" is used to describe a black person who has adopted white society's values; it derives from the name of a servile character in *Uncle Tom's Cabin*. BNE

uniquity *adj.* (unique + iniquity) Singularly wicked, a word allegedly coined to describe New York City. WW

Uniterm *n.* (unit + term) A system of library indexing by which each of a series of documents is made accessible by means of an alphabetical index of subject headings. OED

universanimous *adj.* (universal + unanimous) Being of one mind; unanimous. BL

urbanality *n.* (urbanity + banality) A self-conscious, plodding form of urbanity. Coined by James Thurber. WO

urbanonymous *adj.* (urban + anonymous) Sociological jargon for the condition of isolation and alienation typical of big-city life. JA

urbantry *n.* (urban + country) A rural area which becomes urbanized through development; the suburbs. BAI

urbicide *n.* (urban + suicide) Debilitation of a city through poorly managed development schemes or irresponsible land-use planning. Coined by Wolf Von Eckardt, American architectural critic, in 1966, with a punning reference to **herbicide**. BNE

urinalysis *n.* (urine + analysis) Chemical analysis of the urine. OED

utopiate *n.* (utopia + opiate) A drug which induces a euphoric sense of utopian existence. OED

vanitory *n.* (vanity + lavatory) A bathroom fixture which is a combination lavatory basin and dressing table. WE

Vaporub *brand name* Decongestant vaporizing ointment, Vicks Health Care. BTC

varactor *n.* (varying + reactor) A semiconductor featuring a capacitance which varies with the applied voltage. WE

varistor *n.* (variable + resistor) An electrical resistor with a level of resistance which varies depending upon the applied voltage. WE

vash *n.* (volcanic + ash) Volcanic ash. SWW

vaudevillain *n.* (vaudeville + villain) A humorous colloquial label for a vaudeville performer, otherwise known as a vaudevillian. OED

vegelate *n.* (vegetable + chocolate) Chocolate made with a high concentration of vegetable fats. NW

vegucate *vb.* (vegetable + educate) An effort to inform others about the advantages of vegetarianism. Also: **vegucation.** NW

velveteenager *n.* (velveteen + teenager) A teenager who tends to dress in velvet clothing, a style of dress popular in the 1960s. BAI

Velvetouch *brand name* Christmas decorations, National Tinsel Mfg. Co. BTC

verballistics *n.* (verbal + ballistics) Contentious public discourse in which the participants aim criticism at each other directly or through the media. JO

Versatool *brand name* Screwdrivers, Green Duck Co. BTC

Versatowel *brand name* Paper wipes, Kimberly-Clark Corp. BTC

versiflage *n.* (verse + persiflage) Light verse. BL

Vertebrace *brand name* Extrication collar, Jobst Institute, Inc. BTC

vertebrarterial *adj.* (vertebrate + arterial) Of a vertebra and an artery. OED

vestock *n.* (vest + stock) A clerical collar which extends to the waist. A stock is a piece of material which attaches to a clerical collar and hangs from it. OED

vexasperate *vb.* (vex + exasperate) To exasperate, frustrate or irritate. BL

vibronic *adj.* (vibration + electronic) Pertaining to electronic vibrations and their effects on molecular energy states. DNW

videbut *n.* (video + debut) A debut on television. DNW

videotrocities *n.* (video + atrocities) Particularly offensive examples of mediocre television programming or advertising. WW

vidience *n.* (video + audience) A television audience. YNW

vidiot *n.* (video + idiot) A person obsessed with watching television. TM

vidisk *n.* (video + disc) A type of minifilm movie intended for home viewing. WW

vidozer *n.* (video + dozer) A person who habitually falls asleep while watching television. FW

vindictivolence *n.* (vindictive + malevolence) A desire to avenge oneself or take vengeance. OED

Vinylattice *brand name* Vinyl lattice panels, Cross Vinylattice. BTC

Vinylife *brand name* Vinyl repair kit, M. B. Walton, Inc. BTC

vinylon *n.* (vinyl + nylon) A kind of synthetic fiber which is used in water-resistant fabrics. OED

vinyon *n.* (vinyl + rayon) A manufactured fiber made from synthetic polymers, composed of at least 85 percent vinyl, and having some of the qualities of rayon. DST

Virgilina *n.* (Virginia + Carolina) A city on the border of Virginia and North Carolina. NA

Vitalive *brand name* Fruit bars, Van Melle, Inc. BTC

vitamer *n.* (vitamin + isomer) Certain compounds which relieve a particular vitamin deficiency, an **isomer** being a form of chemical compound. WE

Vitamilk *brand name* Milk, Vitamilk Dairy, Inc. BTC

vitazyme *n.* (vitamin + enzyme) An enzyme, of which one or more components is a vitamin.

vividity *n.* (vivid + avidity) A state of being brashly eager and impatient, a term sometimes used by music critics. BL

vocular *adj.* (vocal + jocular) Disposed to jesting in a loud and irritating fashion. Coined by Charles Dickens.

vodkatini *n.* (vodka + martini) A martini made with vodka instead of gin. BAI

Voicercise *brand name* Prerecorded tapes for developing vocal skills, The Singers Workshop. BTC

voicespond *vb.* (voice + correspond) To correspond by means of re-cordings of spoken messages. OED

volcaniclastic *adj.* (volcanic + clastic) Of or pertaining to a certain type of rock, the origin of which is both volcanic and clastic, clastic rock being made up of fragments of older rock. OED

volumeter *n.* (volume + meter) An instrument for measuring the volume of a gas. WE

volumetric *adj.* (volume + metric) Pertaining to the measurement of volume. WE

vulgularity *n.* (vulgar + popularity) Something which is popular despite — or because of — its inherent vulgarity. BL

waddle *vb.* (wade + toddle) To walk with short steps and a swaying motion. WE

wadge *n.* (wad + wedge) A large, loose bundle; a chunk or heap of matter. STY

Wafrica *n.* (West + Africa) A contraction of **West Africa.** BL

wagery *n.* (wage + slavery) A derisive name for the wage system. OED

wallyball *n.* (wall + volleyball) Volleyball played on a handball court, in which the ball is prevented from going out of play because it bounces off a wall and back onto the court. NWD

wargasm *n.* (war + orgasm) A hypothetical crisis which inevitably leads, in a series of escalating steps, to the climax of nuclear war. DJ

warmedy *n.* (warm + comedy) A film or television program calculated to inspire warm feelings among the audience by its use of patently sentimental material.

warnography *n.* (war + pornography) Any work which tends to glorify war. NW

warphan *n.* (war + orphan) A child orphaned by war. LWW

Waussie *n.* (woman + Aussie) A female member of the Australian Armed Services during World War II. DS

wavicle *n.* (wave + particle) In physics, a physical state exhibiting properties characteristic of both particles and waves. OED

Weedigger *brand name* Lawn and garden tools, Towt Industries. BTC

weeny-bopper *n.* (weeny + teeny-bopper) A pre-adolescent obsessed with following the latest fashions and fads. Weeny-boppers are younger than and thus different from teeny-boppers, **weeny** being used in its diminutive form. Also known as a **tweenager**. BNE

wegotism *n.* (we + egotism) Journalistic slang for excessive use of the editorial **we**. WAW

Westralia *n.* (Western + Australia) The western part of Australia. DS

whang *vb.* (whack + bang) To strike sharply. BL

whirlicane *n.* (whirlwind + hurricane) A hurricane, or any unusually strong windstorm. Coined by American writer Frank Stockton. BL

whirlwig *n.* (whirligig + earwig) Another name for the whirligig beetle. WE

whirry *vb.* (whir + hurry) To hurry. WE

Whitmaniac *n.* (Whitman + maniac) An enthusiast for the American poet Walt Whitman and his work. WE

wholphin *n.* (whale + dolphin) The hybrid of a false killer whale and an Atlantic bottlenose dolphin. TM

whoopla *n.* (whoop + hoopla) A noisy commotion or celebration. WE

whye *n.* (wheat + rye) A hybrid of wheat and rye. ID

widget *n.* (wifflow + gadget) A convenient, offhand designation for any device, contrivance or mechanical gadget. **Wifflow** is also slang for **gadget.** DS

Winchaul *brand name* Winches for sailboats, Asti Products. BTC

Windial *brand name* Wind-speedometer indicator, Airguide Instrument Co. BTC

Winegars *brand name* Cooking wines, Rex Vinegar Co. BTC

winsey *n.* (woolsey + linsey) Plain or twilled fabric with wool weft and cotton or linen warp. WE

winterim *n.* (winter + interim) The interim between semesters at a college or university, usually occurring in January. WES

Winterlude *n.* (winter + interlude) The name given to an annual winter festival in Ottawa, Canada, and elsewhere.

Winterlude *brand name* Carpet, Salem Carpet Mills, Inc. BTC

witticism *n.* (witty + criticism) A witty or clever saying. Coined by poet John Dryden in 1677. YNW

wizzled *adj.* (wizened + shriveled) Wizened and shriveled up. WE

wobbulator *n.* (wobble + modulator) A radio testing device in which the frequency is varied periodically. WE

woggle *vb.* (waggle + wobble) To waggle. WE

womanagement *n.* (woman + management) That which addresses or relates to the particular problems a woman encounters in management positions. BNE

womannequin *n.* (woman + mannequin) A model of the female human body which is used to display women's clothing; a woman who acts the part of a mannequin in a store. JO

womanpower *n.* (woman + manpower) The collective strength or availability of women who are prepared for work. WES

womanthrope *n.* (woman + misanthrope) A hater of women. OED

womoonless *adj.* (woman + moonless) A nonce word coined by James Joyce to describe a panorama or landscape which is particularly dark and desolate. OED

womure *n.* (woman + manure) A gender-modified means of referring to manure. WO

Wonderods *brand name* Fishing equipment, Shakespeare Co. BTC

Woolyester *brand name* Paint rollers, Corona Brushes, Inc. BTC

workfare *n.* (work + welfare) A welfare program in which aid recipients must work, often in public service, to earn their benefits. WES

workoholic *n.* (work + alcoholic) A person obsessed with or addicted to work. DCS

Wraptures *brand name* Leather decorations, Design Circle Ltd. BTC

Wrenaissance *n.* (Wren + Renaissance) A style of architecture influenced by or modeled after the work of Sir Christopher Wren, used particularly in reference to the work of the 20th century English architect Sir Edwin Lutyens. OED

wrizzled *adj.* (wrinkled + frizzled) Shriveled or wrinkled. Coined by the poet Edmund Spenser in *The Faerie Queene*. BAI

wunk *n.* (wasp + funk) A slang term describing the style of teenage music popular in the 1960s. NWD

yabber *vb.* (yack + jabber) To talk incessantly. DS

Yachtwin *brand name* Outboard motors, Evinrude Motors. BTC

yahoomanity *n.* (yahoo + humanity) A derisive name for humanity in general. The word Yahoo was first popularized as a contemptuous name for human beings in Jonathan Swift's *Gulliver's Travels*. BYR

yakalo *n.* (yak + cattalo) The hybrid offspring of a yak and a cattalo. MBD

yakow *n.* (yak + cow) A variety of beef cattle first bred in Great Britain, a hybrid of the common yak and the Highland cow. BNE

Yardarts *brand name* Family lawn game, Eagle Rubber Co., Inc. BTC

yarden *n.* (yard + garden) The plot of land surrounding a house, including its grassy landscaped areas and cultivated garden spaces. FW

Yardener *brand name* Lawn and garden brooms, Empire Brushes, Inc. BTC

yatter *n.* (yammer + chatter) Idle or incessant chatter. TGP

yawn *n.* (yard + lawn) The area of mown grass around a house. FW

yellocution *n.* (yell + elocution) A style of public speaking characterized primarily by the loud voice of the speaker. BL

Yinglish *n.* (Yiddish + English) English words which have been borrowed from Yiddish. Examples include **chutzpah, kibitz, schmuck** and **schlock.** WES

Yogonnaise *brand name* Imitation mayonnaise, Henri's Food Products Co., Inc. BTC

Yogourmet *brand name* Yogurt maker and accessories, VMC Corp. BTC

yonks *n.* (years + months + weeks) British slang for an indefinitely long period of time. DS

Youthair *brand name* Hair coloring, Majestic Drug Co., Inc. BTC

youthquake *n.* (youth + earthquake) The perceived impact of the values and beliefs of the young on established society. WES

yumptious *adj.* (yummy + scrumptious) The nature of something which is especially delicious. BNE

Zappertites *brand name* Microwavable food products, Mayers Food Corp. BTC

zebrass *n.* (zebra + ass) The hybrid of a male zebra and a female ass. WE

zebrule *n.* (zebra + mule) The hybrid of a zebra and a mule. Also spelled **zebrula**. MBD

zedonk *n.* (zebra + donkey) The hybrid offspring of a male zebra and a female donkey. Also known as a **zonkey**. OED

zircalloy *n.* (zirconium + alloy) A zirconium alloy noted for its corrosion resistance and stability when exposed to a wide range of temperatures and radiation levels. Because of its resistance properties, zircalloy is often used as cladding for nuclear reactor fuel rods. WES

zonkey *n.* (zebra + donkey) A zedonk. OED

zumpkin *n.* (zucchini + pumpkin) The hybrid of a zucchini and a pumpkin. SEL

APPENDIX

Advertising and Journalism

abjective, adverteasement, advertique, advertorial, albertype, alibiography, ampersand, anticipointment, bacronym, badvertising, blurb, brandstanding, branwagon, Brisbanality, calligram, camerature, catazine, censcissor, coloroto, commershills, decrassify, educatalog, embargaining, eunanch, euphemantics, expunctuation, fakelore, feevee, flabbergasterisk, gliterary, Herblock, infomaniac, infopreneur, informercial, interrobang, isolite, magalog, mediamorphosis, newspepper, newszine, Newzak, nudgement, opinionnaire, pervertising, plugola, reprography, sexclusive, sexpose, sexpurgate, specialogue, translute, tripewriter, ubookquitous, versiflage, videotrocities, wegotism

Aerospace

ailevator, Airacuda, airmada, airphibian, altazimuth, avigation, balloonatic, ballute, blastard, Canadarm, deceleron, electropult, elevon, flaperon, fleep, flightseeing, flycycle, hangarage, jetevator, judder, loxygen, moondoggle, parasheet, plench, rockoon, ruddervator, satelloon, squadrilla, stabilator, stanine, taileron, transonic, transponder, travelator

Agriculture

agrimation, agrindustry, Ancobar, aphidozer, Australorp, beefalo, Braford, Brangus, Charbray, cowbot, Cubalaya, cultivar, Dorsian, elastration, exclosure, farmerceutical, fertigation, gribble, haylage, matax, nitrogation, organiculture, rotovator, thrinter, twinter, whye, womure

Animals

Ancobar, animule, Australorp, beefalo, Braford, Brangus, camelcade, camelopard, carideer, chaffinch, Charbray, Chessie, churkey, cloof, cockapoo, condorminium, Cubalaya, dorgi, Dorsian, geep, gustard, jackelope, laspring, leopon, liger, mankey, ocicat, pandamonium, petishism, pickering, plantimal, samink, seaquarium, shoat, siabon, slobgollion, snark, splake, swoose, thrinter, tiglon, tigon, tove, trantelope, turken, twinter, whirlwig, wholphin, yakalo, yakow, zebrass, zebrule, zedonk, zonkey

Architectural Design

arcology, autel, barococo, beautility, bellcony, blandscape, cafetorium, Cemestos, condomarinium, condotel, dungalow, ecotecture, edifice complex, electrolier, estatescape, filmosque, gasolier, hometel, Jacobethan, motel, motelodge, odditorium, orchideous, scrolloping, shouse, skylon, smeuse, splanch, squattage, tensegrity, Tudorbethan, Wrenaissance, yarden, yawn

Arts and Literature

applaudience, belletrist, bellygram, bellyrina, bloterature, blottesque, blurb, boffo, booklegger, bovie, boylesk, burletta, camerature, censcissor, crawk, decoreographer, detectifiction, do-pas-so, dramassassins, dramedy, Druriolanus, Emersonthusiast, expectacle, faction, fakelore, gamorous, girlesque, glamazon, gliterary, Grammy, hamateur, heartistic, herohotic, heroicomic, hoggerel, ibsenity, informance, jazzetry, legitimactor, machodrama, mirthquake, mockabre, movelist, Mummerset, Muppet, musicomedy, mythistory, nonsensational, nudancer, orature, pianologue, poet lariat, pornovelist, prequel, radiodor, radiorator, revudeville, revusical, Romiette, scientifiction, sexhibition, sexpurgate, shakesperience, soaperatic, stabile, stencilhouette, stripteuse, tragicomedy, translute, tripewriter, vaudevillain, versiflage, vividity, vulgularity, warnography, Whitmaniac

Attitudes and Behaviors

abstemperous, adaptitude, agreemony, anecdotage, ansurge, anticipointment, applaudience, asiotic, austern, bastich, bestraught, bewilderness, bizark, bletcherous, blunderhead, boobarian, booboisie, brangle, brash, bratitude, brutalitarian, buffion, bullivant, bungaloafer, bungersome, bureausis, cabarazy, celebutante, charitarian, chastigate, chump, clevertivity, compushency, comrogue, confectionate, copelessness, correctitude, corrupie, criticular, dastardice, debutantrum, debutramp, ditsy, doitrified, dooby, dreariment, droob, dumfusion, euphobia, experieak, faddict, fadical, fantigue, fatiloquent, figitated, finickerty, finitiative, flavorite, foolosopher, foozly, frabjous, frumious, frustraneous, fugly, fusty, futilitarian, gamblous, gawkward, geriatrickster, giraffish, giverous, glitterati, glitzy, glumpish, glumpy, glunch, grooly, growsy, grozzle, grum, guestimate, guppie, habitude, half-hazardly, haranag, hective, hellion, heredipity, homocidious, hozey, humaniac, humgumption, ignostic, incestry, infanticipate, insinuendo, intelligentleman, jocoserious, jurisprude, kangarooster, lassitudinarian, lemoncholy, lumbersome, luptious, meacock, meniable, methodolatry, middlescence, mimsy, mingy, mousewife, namesmanship, neatnik, needcessity, nerd, owdacious, oysterics, pecurious, pessimal, petishism, phreak, piffle, platitudinarian, pluranimity, pompass, pompetent, pondynamics, portentious, prissy, profanatic, promptual, psychergy, pushency, querious, racontage, rampallion, rantankerous, rasperated, ritzycratic, roaratorious, routinary, ruckus, rumbumptious, rumbustious, rumption, saccharhinoceros, sanctanimity, sanctimoody, Scandiknavery, scapathy, schooligan, scuzzy, shambolic, sinclination, slimpsy, slimsy, slithy, snazzy, snitzy, snobject, snoblem, solemncholy, somniloquacious, somnorific, Spock-marked, squalmish, squanderlust, swelegant, swelp, systemaniac, Texcentricity, tizzy, tobaccoholic, tobacconalian, touron, tritical, twit, uffish, uniquity, universanimous, urbanality, vexasperate, vindictivolence, vividity, vocular, wizzled, workoholic, wrizzled

Bits and Pieces

blotch, clump, glob, glop, goop, guck, gunk, junt, knurl, mounce, mux, nitch, riffle, shivereens, spetch, splotch, squirk, squirl, twee, wadge

Business and Finance

administralia, administrivia, barsolistor, Bosphorescence, bullionaire, charitarian, Commart, congloperator, corpocracy, diplonomics, echosultant, econometric, enduct, entremanure, entrepreneurtia, Eurocracy, Europhoria, Europort, Eurosclerosis, garbitrageur, groceteria, hesiflation, Honglomerate, identikit, infopreneur, innoventure, methodolatry, millionheiress, monergy, paperalysis, philanthrobber, philanthropoid, recouperation, salariat, sensorship, simoleon, slumpflation, snoopervise, spendacious, squanderlust, stagflation, steelionaire, stockateer, telecommuter, wagery, womanagement, womanpower

Clothing

backini, bitini, bootique, bouffancy, bumbersoll, chemiloon, costumary, curvessence, dresshirt, jingle-bellegant, kerseymere, leotites, meld, moccasock, modacrylic, neatnik, newtique, pantsuit, pettiloon, samink, shagreen, shepherdress, silcott, skort, slopperati, spetch, swacket, tuftaffeta, velveteenager, vestock, vinylon, vinyon, winsey, womannequin

Computers

alphameric, bit, cascode, compunications, computeracy, datamation, experieak, feep, ferrod, glassivation, gubbish, imagineering, magnistor, mechatronics, memistor, metalanguage, molectronics, negentropy, processorhea, sensistor, telecommuter, transputer, twiddle

Crime

blacketeer, booklegger, bootician, buttlegger, Chicagorilla, gayola, goon, Hawcubites, homocidious, hoolivan, Identikit, meatlegger, philanthrobber, phreak, prevaricaterer, schooligan, scissorean, skyjack, smothercate, squadrol, sweedle

Drug Slang

blort, brutal nitrate, Hashbury, jolly bean, maridelic, marijuanaful, psychedelicatessan, Psychedelphia, utopiate

Education

acceleread, bratitude, bugology, communiversity, computeracy, educant, Educare, educrat, examnesia, fratority, juvenescence, libratory, multiversity, niniversity, numeracy, oracy, Oxbridge, schooligan, scollage, sorernity, stanine, transescent, Uniterm, winterim

Figures of Speech

altiloquence, ambiloquence, bladderdash, blandiloquence, bloviate, blurt, bomfog, brangle, breviloquence, bromidiom, camouflanguage, cangle, chackle, chastigate, chipe, clacket, duologue, explaterate, flamdoodle, fuzzword, haranag, jawbation, jivernacular, magniloquent, noration, parlambling, piffle, platitudinarian, racontage, radiorator, sejole, sleer, soliloquacity, soliloquery, somniloquacious, splather, squabash, stultiloquence, testiculating, verballistics, vocular, voicespond, yabber, yatter, yellocution

Food and Drink

alegar, aniseed, biscake, blandlubber, broast, broccoflower, brunch, bruncheon, brunner, butterine, canola, caraburger, carnibbleous, carnivoracity, celtuce, chessel, chocoholic, choff, citrange, clamburger, colaholic, craisin, croissandwich, cruisine, daiquirita, delushious, dunch, epicurate, fizzician, flavory, frickles, frizzle, fruice, garlion, gasid, gastronomer, gingerine, gorp, groceteria, grozzle, guttle, jamocha, jollop, lactalbumin, lamburger, limequat, limon, lumpshious, luncheon, lupper, macon, meatlegger, mexicola, mocktail, nutarian, nutter, orangelo, oranghetti, ovalbumin, oysterics, plumcot, prevaricaterer, pursley, saketini, seatron, shamburger, shampagne, smores, spork, stewp, stuffocation, swilge, tangelo, tilge, tinner, vegelate, vegucate, vodkatini, yumptious

Gender Blenders

ambisextrous, boil, boylesk, bubby, concubub, facho, femagoguery, Femarines, femcee, feminar, fumorist, galimony, gayola, harumphrodite, hermaphrodite, herstory, hesh, hir, hirm, Manglish, palimony, shedonism, shemale, shero, shim, sothers, thon, womanagement, womannequin, womanpower, womanthrope, womure

Geography

Arkahoma, Birome, Calexico, Calneva, Canalaska, Centrahoma, Centralia, Chunnel, Dakoming, Delkaria, Eastralia, Elmonica, Florala, hempire, Kanorado, Kensee, Kentuckiana, Mesopolonica, Metrollopis, Mexicali, Michillinda, Minniapple, Neurope, Newfanglia, Norlina, Nosodak, Ohiowa, Oxbridge, peninsularity, Psychedelphia, quaggy, Senegambia, swallet, Tanzania, terraqueous, Texarkana, Texico, Virgilina, Wafrica, Westralia

Geology

dingot, Earthoon, fanglomerate, felsic, jasponyx, Moorth, palevent, sandust, solunar, surficial, tremblor, vash, volcaniclastic

Industry

airdraulic, albertype, alundum, ampacity, austempering, bitumastic, blunge, bulgine, carbecue, Carboloy, catapunch, cellophane, Cemestos, ceramagnet, ceramal, chemagination, chemiluminescence, chemonomics, chemurgy, compregnate, coulometer, deformeter, dynamotor, electromatic, enduct, epoxidation, extreamline, fagtory, fluorod, galvanneal, glassivation, glowboy, gription, handraulic, handtector, heatronic, humanation, hygristor, identikit, imagineering, immittance, latensification, lunk, magnalium, magnetron, manit, martempering, mechatronics, meld, milliammeter, mobot, molectronics, Nichrome, nife, petroil, photronic, plench, prillion, pritchel, reprography, sensistor, silumin, stator, telephonograph, tensegrity, thermistor, tricknology, zircalloy

Inebriation

abstemperous, alcoholiday, beerocracy, beerstro, biffy, binge, blunk, boozician, daiquirita, dipsy, drunch, foozly, fruice, gingerine, impixlocated, inebriety, jollop, mexicola, mocktail, saketini, saloonatic, scooch, shampagne, swizzle, vodkatini

Language

Amerenglish, Americanecdote, Anglistics, bacronym, Borotuke, Chicargot, Coca-Colonialism, daffynition, dingle, epigrammar, Franglais, Frenglish, fuzzword, Hinglish, homonymble, jargantuan, jargonaut, jargoneer, jivernacular, malaphor, Manglish, orature, perverb, phonestheme, portmantologism, processorhea, profanatic, reversicon, shitticism, Singlish, slang, slanguage, slangular, Spanglish, Spinnish, Swinglish, telephonetics, witticism, Yinglish

Medicine and Health

abortuary, adrenergic, airbrasive, apprehendicitis, blunk, bubukle, bulimarexia, caplet, clinicar, cosmoceutical, dermabrasion, dormantory, elastration, extencisor, feebility, fluidram, gasid, humalin, lassitudinarian, Medicare, medichair, narcoma, obstipation, parafango, parathormone, pelviscope, periphlebitis, pindling, pinlay, pulmonia, Pulmotor, quackupuncture, screwmatics, scringe, sexpert, sicklemia, skinjury, smotheration, spansule, stuffocation, tenigue, tobaccoholic, urinalysis, vertebrarterial, vitamer

Military

Airacuda, airmada, airtillery, armoraider, atomaniac, balloonatic, blastard, bomphlet, Bren, camelry, chairborne, Femarines, gaspirator, gungineer, gyrene, humint, Japanazi, Mesopolonica, milicrat, napalm, nukemare, parashoot, racon, radome, roblitz, robomb, scapathy, scrapnel, seavacuation, seep, smatchet, Sovietnam, squadrilla, terrorilla, wargasm, warnography, warphan, Waussie

Miscellaneous

candelabracadabra, conclusory, dang, evidentually, Global Releaf, gormagon, herodynamics, horrorscope, irregardless, klavern, kleagle, klonclave, Klonvocation, Kloran, Mexicancellation, occultivated, pinkermint, plumpendicular, pother, randem, rapidry, repristination, saucerer, scrowsy, slantindicular, slightually, squdgy, thoughtography, transparesscent, ufocal, uforia, womoonless, yahoomanity

Motor Transport

Africar, airphibian, autel, autobesity, automobility, autopia, Bakerloo, blowmobile, bulgine, buscapade, clinicar, diesohol, fuelish, gasohol, grice, gridlock, gription, jeepney, motel, motelodge, motopia, motorail, motorama, motorcade, Motown, petroil, replicar, rimbellisher, roadeo, scrutineer, seep, smokolotive, squadrol, trafficator, truppie

Movies and Television

animatronics, anticipointment, Batmania, blacksploitation, Blacula, boffo, Bondoggle, bovie, camerantics, cinemactress, cinemaddict, cinemagpie, cinemalefactor, cinemammoth, cinemaniac, cinemenace, cinemogul, commershills, docutainment, dramedy, earjerker, eroduction, eunanch, expectacle, feevee, filmosque, gamorous, Gidget, glamazon, Hollywoodenhead, informercial, infotainment, inscrewtable, isolite, kidult, legitimactor, machodrama, Manimal, mediamorphosis, mirthquake, movelist, movideo, Muppet, Newzak, nickelodeon, peekture, Pickfair, plugola, prequel, psychiatricky, rockumentary, Sensurround, sexploitation, sexport, sinema, skitcom, soaperatic, telectorate, telegogue, televangelist, televisionary, trialevision, videbut, videotrocities, vidience, vidiot, vidisk, vidozer, warmedy

Music

abusak, bandstration, banjoey, banjolin, banjorine, banjulele, baritenor, Beatles, blastissimo, burletta, cassingle, cittern, clavicylinder, claviola, earjerker, Elvisitor, flarp, Grammy, harmolodic, harmonicello, infernoise, jazzetry, leerics, lyrichord, melodica, Motown, movideo, musicassette, musicomedy, organola, orpharion, pianologue, revudeville, revusical, rockabilly, rockappella, rockumentary, sexophone, singspiration, soundscape, tamboo, tenoroon, vividity, wunk

Nautical

boatel, canoodle, cargador, Chessie, coastel, condomarinium, crough, cruisine, floatel, garbarge, lasket, marline, portledge, riffle, seafari, seavacuation, seep

Ordinary Things

anticer, beezer, belkupping, bingle, brinkles, bumbersoll, camporee, cellophane, chairoplane, cigaroot, cocomat, contraption, cremains, derbish, flare, fuzzstache, gimp, gollywog, grice, guzunder, happenstance, hellophone, hintimation, hokum, Jewfro, kissletoe, manscape, matax, milkstache, newelty, newt, pajamboree, pang, pantler, pentagle, photomaton, planacea, pockmanteau, rubbage, sennight, shifferobe, simoleon, slench, sloosh, sneakret, soroptimist, sparcity, squiz, striggle, stringlet, surroundry, sweatspiration, testificate, tosh, travelator, travelogue, trendency, tweenager, twinsult, twirligig, vanitory, weeny-bopper, widget, womannequin, workoholic, yarden, yawn, yonks

People

Aframerican, Afrasian, Amerasian, Amerindian, Australasian, Baltimorons, Eurafrican, Eurasian, Louisvillain, Madhattaner, Michigander, Naussie, Newyorican, Omahogs, Randlord, refujew, Scowegian, Shanghailander, Texican

Plants

azaleamum, broccoflower, cabatoe, canola, celtuce, citrange, garlion, hican, kaferita, kissletoe, limequat, limon, mosaiculture, nicotunia, orangelo, oranghetti, orchideous, ortanique, pepperidge, plantimal, plumcot, pomato, potomato, pursley, tangelo, tangemon, tangor, topato, topepo, triticale, vegucate, whye, zumpkin

Politics and Government

aldermanity, alphabetterment, Americaid, atomaniac, barnacular, bloviate, bomfog, boobocracy, brutalitarian, bureaucrap, bureaucrazy, bureaucrock, bureausis, camouflanguage, carcinomenclature, commyrot, compossible, crant, dawk, democrapic, diplonomics, Dixican, Dixiecrats, donkophant, echosultant, electionomics, extrality, factrip, fadical, gerrymander, globaloney, Goldwaterloo, groupuscule, guestage, humaniac, Indocrat, irage, Judicare, McGovernment, Medicare, Moosevelt, Neurope, obscureaucrat, Peterloo, philanthropoid, pluranimity, politichine, politricks, pollitician, povertician, prinister, Prohiblican, quetopia, radicalesbian, Reagonomics, refujew, Republocrat, selectorate, sensorship, Sovietnam, spendacious, Spinnish, telectorate, terrorilla, tissue, Ulsteria, Uncle Tomahawk, workfare

Religion

archaeolatry, bathtize, churchianity, demonagerie, ecumaniac, epicurate, gloriole, goditorium, hellennium, idylatry, ignostic, lordolatry, magpiety, Newmania, nobodaddy, popestant, presbygational, priestianity, profanatic, sacerdotage, sanctanimity, sanctimoody, singspiration, squarson, squishop, symbolatry, taboobery, tarnation, televangelist, vestock

Science and Technology

acutangular, alphametic, astrometry, atomechanics, avigation, bacterinert, bugology, Canadarm, cascode, chemagination, chemiluminescence, chemurgy, circannual, climatype, compander, conceptacle, coulometer, cubangle, cybot, dynamotor, electret, enduct, environics, epoxidation, extreamline, fluorod, funginert, glassivation, graser, heatronic, humalin, huminal, hygristor, immittance, imperviable, integraph, kip, lactalbumin, latensification, libratory, lidar, loxygen, magnetron, magnistor, manit, mathemagician, mattergy, meaconing, memistor, milliammeter, molectronics, mounce, negatron, negentropy, nucleonics, numberal, olfactronics, opacifier, ovalbumin, parathormone, pervaporation, photronic, planetesimal, positron, pulsar, racon, rectenna, rockoon, sensistor, sodar, soliquid, solunar, stellarator, stiction, surfactant, toxicyst, transceiver, transfection, transistor, transonic, transverter, tricknology, troposcatter, ubiquinone, ultraviolation, varactor, varistor, vibronic, vitamer, vitazyme, voicespond, volumeter, volumetric, wavicle, wobbulator

Sexuality

ambisextrous, bluff, curfloozie, curvessence, dingle, ecstatician, entreporneur, eroduction, funch, gonocide, hobosexual, hozey, incestry, inscrewtable, leerics, lewdity, lovertine, patriotute, peekture, pervertising, phallacy, pinkler, playbore, poncess, pornicator, pornovelist, prostisciutto, radicalesbian, rendezwoo, sexational, sexcapade, sexclusive, sexercise, sexetary, sexhibition, sexophone, sexpert, sexplanatory, sexplicit, sexploitation, sexplosion, sexport, sexpose, sexpurgate, sextrovert, shemale, sinclination, sinema, sinsational, smorgasborgy, swingle, taboobery

Shakespeare

Ariachne, Bakespeare, bardolatry, Druriolanus, impittious, intrinsicate, rebuse, Romiette, Shaconian, shakesperience, triumpherate

Sociology

Americaid, arcology, autopia, beerage, birthquake, boobocracy, booboisie, californicate, charitarian, chuppie, compossible, corrupie, Democracity, dingle, droppie, ecotage, ecumenopolis, environmental illness, foppy, glitterati, groupuscule, guppie, hobohemia, huppie, megalopolitan, Metrollopis, metropollyana, metropolypus, motopia, Newfanglia, paltripolitan, populuxe, povertician, proprietariat, queutopia, rurban, salariat, siberbia, sloburb, slub, slurb, snivelization, Spock-marked, subtopia, truppie, Uncle Tomahawk, urbanonymous, urbantry, urbicide, workfare, youthquake

Sports and Recreation

Bosox, camporee, canogganing, canoodle, cricketiquette, dancercise, decathlete, dolfan, doubleton, extencisor, femlin, foozle, frontenis, golfelt, gumbacco, huskiing, immateur, jarming, Mardi Grass, maximin, Octopush, Paralympics, parascending, polocrosse, ringoal, roleo, runagade, scrutineer, scurb, seafari, sexercise, shamateurism, skatebordello, skiddles, skish, skitching, skurfing, slickery, Slimnastics, snofari, snurfing, splork, superfecta, surfari, threepeat, trainasium, triathlete, triggernometry, tumblesault, twinight, umperor, wallyball, Winterlude

Superlatives

abhorrible, abnormous, absolete, baffound, begincement, bizotic, bodacious, clantastical, cornucopious, cruical, delushious, disastrophe, dwizzened, exaccurate, fandangled, fantabulous, frabjous, ginormous, grandacious, grandificent, humongous, jargantuan, magniloquent, momentaneous, monstracious, numberous, owdacious, plentitude, posolutely, roaratorious, savagerous, scandiculous, smelodious, torrible, tremense, universanimous, whoopla, yumptious

Weather

chizzly, drismal, drizzerable, flurry, foggle, fozzle, glime, grismal, gusterly, hain, himmicane, hoke, humiture, mizzle, mugid, smaze, smice, smist, smog, smoud, smurk, smust, snain, sneet, snirt, snoud, sposh, sprinter, squoggy, sweltry, thumble, torrible, whirlicane, winterim

Words Indicating Action

aggranoy, aggrovoke, argle, argufy, baffound, bash, blash, bonk, boost, brustle, californicate, cangle, canoodle, chortle, chuff, clash, clunch, correctify, cramble, crinch, croodle, crowl, dandle, depicture, doddle, doff, don, draggle, dripple, dumbfound, electrocute, embrangle, expugn, flabbergast, flaunt, flether, flimmer, flisk, flop, flounder, flounge, flump, flunk, flush, flusticate, flustrate, foozle, fustle, galumph, gimble, grasple, graunch, gribble, gritch, gropple, grozzle, grubble, grumble, gummixed, guttle, hassle, huggle, itchitate, jummix, maddle, matterate, meld, mizzle, mog, mudge, natter, nursle, peacify, piffle, piroot, plodge, possibilitate, preliminate, previnder, prickado, pringle, prod, prounce, rebuse, recomember, rollick, rumfle, satisfice, scamble, scance, scarify, scrawl, scraze, scriggle, scringe, scrumble, scrump, scrumple, scrunch, scutter, scuttle, slather, slidder, slosh, slurch, smarm, smash, smothercate, snangle, snicker, snitter, snoozle, snuzzle, sojourney, splather, splatter, splosh, splunge, splurge, splutter, squash, squench, squiggle, squinch, squish, squnch, stramp, strome, studdle, suspose, swash, sweedle, swipe, swizzle, thumble, thwack, tipple, trampede, trampoose, tromp, twiddle, twindle, twirl, waddle, whang, whirry, woggle

BIBLIOGRAPHY

Barlough, Ernest J. *The Archaicon*. Metuchen, N.J.: Scarecrow, 1974.

Barnhart, Clarence L. *The Barnhart Dictionary Companion*. Cold Spring, N.Y.: Lexik House, 1987.

_____. *The Barnhart Dictionary of New English Since 1963*. Bronxville, N.Y.: Barnhart/Harper & Row, 1973.

_____. *The Second Barnhart Dictionary of New English*. Bronxville, N.Y.: Barnhart/Harper & Row, 1980.

Barnhart, Robert K., Sol Steinmetz and Clarence L. Barnhart. *The Barnhart Dictionary of New English*. New York: H. W. Wilson, 1990.

Berg, Paul C. *A Dictionary of New Words in English*. London: George Allen & Unwin, 1953.

Black, Donald Chain. *Spoonerisms, Sycophants & Sops*. New York: Harper & Row, 1988.

Brandreth, Gyles. *The Joy of Lex*. New York: William Morrow, 1980.

_____. *The Pears Book of Words*. London: Pelham Books, 1979.

Bryant, Margaret M. "Blends Are Increasing," *American Speech*, Volume 49, Spring-Summer, 1974.

Burchfield, R. W. *A Supplement to the Oxford English Dictionary*. Oxford: Clarendon, 1972.

Byrne, Josefa Heifetz. *Mrs. Byrne's Dictionary*. Secaucus, N.J.: Citadel Press, 1974.

Chapman, Robert L. *New Dictionary of American Slang*. New York: Harper & Row, 1986.

Ciardi, John. *A Browser's Dictionary*. New York: Harper & Row, 1980.

_____. *A Second Browser's Dictionary*. New York: Harper & Row, 1983.

Dickson, Paul. *Family Words*. Reading, Mass.: Addison-Wesley, 1988.

_____. *Names*. New York: Delacorte, 1986.

_____. *Slang*. New York: Pocket Books, 1990.

_____. *Words*. New York: Delacorte, 1982.

Dohan, Mary Helen. *Our Own Words*. New York: Alfred A. Knopf, 1974.

Evans, Ivor H. *Brewer's Dictionary of Phrase & Fable*. New York: Harper & Row, 1981.

Firebaugh, Joseph. "The Vocabulary of Time Magazine," *American Speech*, Volume XV, 1940.

Fisher, John. *The Magic of Lewis Carroll*. New York: Simon & Schuster, 1973.

Flexner, Stuart Berg. *I Hear America Talking*. New York: Simon & Schuster, 1976.

Freeman, Morton S. *The Story Behind the Word*. Philadelphia: ISI, 1985.

Gardner, Martin. *The Annotated Alice*. New York: Bramhall House, 1960.

Gove, Philip Babcock, ed. *Webster's 3rd International Dictionary*. Springfield, Mass.: G & C Merriam, 1971.

Grambs, David. *Words About Words*. New York: McGraw-Hill, 1984.

Green, Jonathon. *The Dictionary of Contemporary Slang*. Stein & Day, 1985.

_____. *Newspeak: A Dictionary of Jargon*. London: Routledge & Kegan Paul, 1984.

Hellweg, Paul. *The Insomniac's Dictionary*. New York: Facts on File, 1986.

Hendrickson, Robert. *American Talk*. New York: Viking Penguin, 1986.

Homer, Joel. *Jargon*. New York: Times Books, 1979.

Hook, J. N. *The Grand Panjandrum*. New York: Macmillan, 1980.

Hudson, Derek. *Lewis Carroll*. London: Constable, 1954.

Laird, Carlton. *The Word*. New York: Simon & Schuster, 1981.

Lambdin, William. *Doublespeak Dictionary*. Los Angeles, Cal.: Pinnacle, 1979.

Lemay, Harold, Sid Lerner and Marian Taylor. *New Words Dictionary*. New York: Ballantine, 1985.

_____. *New Words Dictionary*. New York: Ballantine, 1988.

McAdam, E. L. and George Milne, eds. *Johnson's Dictionary: A Modern Selection*. London: Macmillan, 1982.

McCrum, Robert, William Cran and Robert McNeil. *The Story of English*. New York: Elisabeth Sifton Books–Viking, New York, 1986.

Mager, N. H. and S. K. Mager *Morrow Book of New Words*. New York: William Morrow, 1982.

Marckwardt, Albert H. *American English*. New York: Oxford University Press, 1958.

Marcuse, Sibyl. *Musical Instruments*. New York: W. W. Norton, 1975.

Mencken, H. L. *The American Language*. New York: Alfred A. Knopf, 1936.

Miller, Don Ethan. *The Book of Jargon*. New York: Macmillan, 1981.

Mish, Frederick C., ed. *12,000 Words, A Supplement to Webster's Third New International Dictionary*. Springfield, Mass.: Merriam-Webster, 1986.

Morris, William, ed. *The American Heritage Dictionary of the English Language*. Boston: Houghton Mifflin, 1979.

_____ and Mary Morris. *Harper Dictionary of Contemporary Usage*. New York: Harper & Row, 1975.

_____ and Mary Morris. *Morris Dictionary of Word and Phrase Origins*. New York: Harper & Row, 1977.

Mort, Simon, ed. *Longman Guardian New Words*. Essex, England: Longman, 1986.

Parker, Sybil P., editor-in-chief. *The McGraw-Hill Dictionary of Scientific and Technical Terms*. New York: McGraw-Hill, 1984.

Partridge, Eric. *A Dictionary of Slang and Unconventional English*. New York: Macmillan, 1984.

_____. *Slang Today and Yesterday*. New York: Macmillan, 1950.

Pei, Mario. *Doublespeak in America*. New York: Hawthorn, 1973.

_____. *The Story of Language*. Philadelphia: J. B. Lippincott, 1965.

_____. *The Story of the English Language*. Philadelphia: J. P. Lippincott, 1967.

_____. *Weasel Words*. New York: Harper & Row, 1978.

_____. *Words in Sheep's Clothing*. New York: Hawthorn, 1969.

Poister, John J. *The New American Bartender's Guide*. New York: New American Library, 1989.

Pound, Louise. "Blends: Their Relation to English Word Formation," *Anglistische Forschungen,* Vol. 42, 1914.

_____. "Indefinite Composites and Word-Coinage," *Modern Language Review,* 1913.

Pyles, Thomas. *Words & Ways of American English*. New York: Random House, 1952.

Rawson, Hugh. *A Dictionary of Euphemism & Other Doubletalk*. New York: Crown, 1981.

Reifer, Mary. *Dictionary of New Words*. New York: Philosophical Library, 1955.

Rocke, Russell. *The Grandiloquent Dictionary*. Englewood Cliffs, N.J.: Prentice-Hall, 1972.

Root, Waverly. *Food*. New York: Simon & Schuster, 1980.

Rosenberg, Jerry M. *Dictionary of Computer Data Processing and Telecommunications*. New York: John Wiley & Sons, 1984.

Safire, William. *I Stand Corrected*. New York: The New York Times Book Co., 1984.

_____. *On Language*. New York: The New York Times Book Co., 1980.

_____. *What's the Good Word?* New York: The New York Times Book Co., 1982.

Saussy, George Stone, III. *The Oxter English Dictionary*. New York: Facts on File, 1984.

Scheuer, Steven H. *Movies on TV*. Toronto: Bantam, 1987.

Sherk, William. *Brave New Words*. Toronto: Doubleday, 1979.

_____. *500 Years of New Words*. Toronto: Doubleday, 1983.

_____. *More Brave New Words*. Toronto: Doubleday, 1981.

Shipley, Joseph T. *In Praise of English*. New York: The New York Times Book Co., 1977.

Simpson, J. A. and E. S. C. Weiner. *The Oxford English Dictionary*. 2d edition. Oxford: Clarendon, 1989.

Spears, Richard A. *NTC's Dictionary of Slang and Colloquial Expressions*. Lincolnwood, Ill.: National Textbook, 1990.

Stewart, George R. *Names on the Land.* New York: Random House, 1945.

Success with Words. Pleasantville, N.Y.: Reader's Digest, 1983.

Taylor, A. Margaret. *The Language of World War II.* New York: H. W. Wilson, 1948.

Tucker, Gilbert M. *American English.* New York: Alfred A. Knopf, 1921.

Wagner, Geoffrey. *On the Wisdom of Words.* Princeton, N.J.: D. Von Nostrand, 1968.

Walker, Lester. *American Shelter.* Woodstock, N.Y.: Overlook, 1981.

Wentworth, Harold, and Stuart Berg Flexner. *Dictionary of American Slang.* New York: Thomas Y. Crowell, 1975.

Wood, Donna, ed. *Brands and Their Companies.* Detroit: Gale Research, 1991.

_____. *Trade Names Dictionary.* 6th edition. Detroit: Gale Research, 1988.

Yates, Norris. "The Vocabulary of Time Magazine Revisited," *American Speech,* Volume 56, 1981.